I0682284

ODD

AMY LE FEUVRE

Odd

Amy Le Feuvre

© 1st World Library, 2009
PO Box 2211
Fairfield, IA 52556
www.1stworldlibrary.com
First Edition

LCCN: 2009923335

Softcover ISBN: 978-1-4218-8807-1
Hardcover ISBN: 978-1-4218-8906-1
eBook ISBN: 978-1-4218-8708-1

Purchase *"Odd"*
as a traditional bound book at:
www.1stWorldLibrary.com/purchase.asp?ISBN=978-1-4218-8807-1

1st World Library is a literary, educational organization
dedicated to:

- Creating a free internet library of downloadable ebooks

- Hosting writing competitions and offering book publishing
  scholarships.

1st World Library Literary Society

Giving Back to the World

"If you want to work on the core problem, it's early school literacy."

- James Barksdale, former CEO of Netscape

"No skill is more crucial to the future of a child, or to a democratic and prosperous society, than literacy."

- Los Angeles Times

"Literacy... means far more than learning how to read and write... The aim is to transmit... knowledge and promote social participation."

- UNESCO

"Literacy is not a luxury, it is a right and a responsibility. If our world is to meet the challenges of the twenty-first century we must harness the energy and creativity of all our citizens."

- President Bill Clinton

"Parents should be encouraged to read to their children, and teachers should be equipped with all available techniques for teaching literacy, so the varying needs and capacities of individual kids can be taken into account."

- Hugh Mackay

CONTENTS

CHAPTER I. CAGED BIRDS......................7

CHAPTER II. 'MOTHER NATURE'......................16

CHAPTER III. WAS IT AN ANGEL?......................26

CHAPTER IV. ADVENTURES......................37

CHAPTER V. PRINCE 50

CHAPTER VI. MADE INTO A COUPLE......................61

CHAPTER VII. HAYMAKING......................73

CHAPTER VIII. GOD'S PATCHWORK......................82

CHAPTER IX. BETTY'S DISCOVERY......................92

CHAPTER X. A LITTLE MESSENGER......................103

CHAPTER XI. A DARING FEAT......................112

CHAPTER XII. UNCLE HARRY'S FRIEND......................123

CHAPTER XIII. 'WHEN WE TWO MET'......................132

CHAPTER XIV. A HERO'S DEATH 144

CHAPTER XV. COMFORTED 154

CHAPTER I

CAGED BIRDS

It was just four o'clock on a dull grey winter afternoon. The little Stuarts' nursery looked the picture of cosiness and comfort with the blazing fire that threw flickering lights over the bright-coloured pictures on the walls, the warm carpet under foot, and the fair fresh faces of the children gathered there.

Five of them there were, and they were alone, for the old nurse who had brought them all up from their infancy was at present absent from the room.

By one of the large square windows stood one of the little girls; she was gazing steadily out into the fast darkening street below, her chin resting on one of the bars that were fastened across the lower part of the window. How the children disliked those bars! Marks of little teeth were plainly discernible along them, and no prisoners could have tried more perseveringly to shake them from their sockets than they did. Betty, who stood there now, had received great applause one afternoon when, after sundry twists and turns, she had successfully thrust her little dark curly head through, and was able to have a delightfully clear view of all the passers-by.

But the sequel was not so pleasant, for somehow or other Betty's head would not come in so easily as it went out, and when nurse came to the rescue with an angry hand, the poor little head was very much bruised in consequence, and Betty's reward for such dexterity was an aching head and dry bread for tea. She was a slight, slim little figure, with big blue eyes, and long, black curved lashes and eyebrows, which made her eyes the most beautiful feature in her face. Very soft, fine curly hair surrounded a rather pathetic-looking little face; but her movements were like quicksilver, and though all the little Stuarts were noted for their mischievous ways and daring escapades, Betty eclipsed them all.

She turned from the window soon with a sigh of relief.

'He's coming,' she said, 'old Bags is coming, and it's my turn to-day.'

There was no response. Bobby and Billy, the twins, little lads only just promoted from petticoats to knickerbockers, were deeply engrossed in one corner of the room over their bricks. Perched on the top of a low chest of drawers were Douglas and Molly, and their heads were in that close proximity that told that secret business was going on.

Betty's heart sank a little.

'Old Bags is coming,' she repeated; 'don't you hear his bell?'

'We're busy,' said Douglas, looking up; 'we won't have Bags' story to-day.'

'You promised yesterday when you put it off that you would hear it to-day. It isn't fair. I always listen to you.'

'Tell it to the babies; they'll like to hear.'

This was adding insult to injury, and when the twins trotted up to the window Betty turned a defiant back upon them, tears of disappointment dimming the blue eyes.

'She's cwying,' announced Bobby, twisting his head round to look up into her face.

Betty turned round furiously; a sharp push sent Bobby to the ground, and in falling he struck his head against one of the feet of the nursery table. There was a howl, general confusion, and nurse appeared, to discover and chastise the offender. Betty was led off in disgrace to a little room on the nursery landing, known by the children as 'Cells.' Their uncle, a young captain in the Guards, had given it that name, but in reality it was nurse's storeroom, and was heated with hot pipes, to air the linen kept there. It was a small, square room, containing a table and one chair; the window was high above the children's reach, and locked cupboards were on every side. Nurse invariably used it for punishing small offences, and being a woman of stern principles, she generally set the little culprit a text to learn whilst there. A Bible was on the table, and Betty was led up to it.

'You will stay here till tea-time, and will not come out until you have learnt a text, and said you are sorry for knocking down your little brother in a fit of wicked temper. This is the fourth time I have had to bring you here this week, and it is now only Tuesday. I have more trouble with you than all the others put together, and you ought to be ashamed of yourself.'

Betty was sobbing bitterly, and when nurse left the room and turned the key behind her, the child flung herself down on the floor.

'It's a shame! It's all Douglas and Molly: they make promises and don't keep them; and it was ever so much nicer a story than Molly's. I know they'd have liked it if they'd heard it; they never think I can do anything!'

To explain the cause of Betty's grievance, I must tell you that it was a custom of the little Stuarts to await the muffin man's approach on his rounds, and as his bell would sound, they would take it in turns each day to relate to the others an account of the different houses he had gone to, and who had been the fortunate individuals to receive the muffins that had already disappeared from his tray. It was an idle hour in the nursery from four to five, and if the gathering dusk kept the active eyes still, the fertile brains were brought into requisition. Telling stories was a constant delight, and the wonderful adventures that befell the muffins on their daily rounds kept the little gathering quiet and happy till tea appeared.

Betty's stories were not inferior to her elders, and it was her childish sense of justice and consideration that was outraged. But tears will come to an end, and soon the little maiden was perched up at the table to learn the task before her. She turned over the pages till she reached Revelation, that mysterious and mystical book that so fascinates and contents a child's soul, though the wisest on earth read it with perplexity and awe. And after a moment or two Betty had found a text to learn, and when nurse appeared later on she repeated unfalteringly with shining eyes and with a note of triumph in her tone 'And I said unto him, Sir, thou knowest. And he said to me, These are they which came out of great tribulation, and have washed their robes, and made them white in the blood of the Lamb' (Rev. vii. 14).

'That's a good child; are you sorry?'

'Yes,' was the reply, rather absently given, for Betty's mind was on the white-robed throng; and how could she let nurse know all the workings of her busy brain over the verse she had been taking into her heart and soul?

'And remember,' said nurse gravely, 'that no naughty children who quarrel and fight will ever be in heaven.'

'Not even if they've been through great tribulation?' quickly demanded Betty.

But nurse did not hear, and Betty was received into the well-lighted nursery with acclamation from the others, already seated at the round table for tea.

'We've made a new game, Molly and I,' announced Douglas.

He was a fair, curly-headed boy with an innocent baby face, and a talent for inventing the most mischievous plans that could ever be concocted, with a will that made all the others bow before him. Molly was also fair, with long golden hair that reached to her waist; extreme self-possession and absence of all shyness were perhaps her chief characteristics. 'I am the eldest of the family,' she was fond of asserting, and she certainly claimed the eldest's privileges. Yet her temper was sweet and obliging, and she could easily be swayed and led by those around her.

'Is it one for outdoors or indoors?' asked Betty with interest.

'Indoors, of course; we'll tell you after tea.'

'Your mother wants you in the drawing-room after ten,' put in nurse; 'you and Miss Molly are to go down.'

Molly looked pleased, not so Douglas. At last, putting down his piece of bread and butter, he looked up into nurse's face with one of his sweetest looks.

'Why are grown-up people so very dull, nurse? They all are just the same, except Uncle Harry. They are dreadfully heavy and dull.'

'They have so little to amuse them,' Molly said reflectively: 'no games or toys; they never make believe, or pretend the lovely things we do.'

'And their legs get stiff, and their dresses trip them up if they try to run.'

'But they never get punished, and they're never scolded, and they're never wicked.'

This from Betty.

'It's their talk that is so stupid,' went on Douglas; 'they look nice until they begin to talk; they make me dreadfully sleepy to listen to them.'

'Shall I go down instead of you to-night?' asked Betty eagerly.

'Don't chatter such nonsense; it's strange times when children begin to pick their elders to pieces. You weren't asked for, Miss Betty; and Master Douglas is to go down and behave himself.'

'The three B's aren't big enough yet to leave the nursery.'

Douglas said this with a sparkle of mischief in his eye. It was a sore point with Betty to be ranked with the twins, for she was only a year behind Douglas. Long ago he had seized hold of a laughing joke of his father's, alluding to the names by which the three youngest children were called, and had twitted her with it ever since.

'B for Baby—Baby Betty, Baby Bobby, and Baby Billy; babies must go to bed,' he explained.

Betty gave an angry kick under the table, but did not speak.

She was very silent for the rest of that evening; but when she and Molly were safely in bed, and the room was very quiet, she asked,—

'Molly, do you know what tribulation means?'

'I'm not sure that I do,' was the hesitating reply; 'I think it's something dreadful. Why do you want to know?'

'Is it like the dark valley Christian went through in the *Pilgrim's Progress*, or the goblin's cave we make up about?'

'I expect it is something like. Why?'

'It's on the way to heaven,' whispered Betty, in an awestruck tone; 'the Bible says so.'

There was silence, then Molly said,—

'There's a book in father's library will tell you about it. It tells the meaning of every word; father said so. A dick something it is.'

'I'll ask Mr. Roper to get it for me.'

And Betty turned over on her pillow comforted by this thought, and fell fast asleep.

Mr. Stuart was a Member of Parliament, and being a man who threw his whole soul into everything he did, was too much engrossed with business when in town to have much to do with his children. He spent a great part of his day in the library with his secretary, a quiet young fellow, who was looked upon by the children as an embodiment of wisdom and learning. Mrs. Stuart saw as little of her children as her husband; her time was fully occupied in attending committee meetings, opening bazaars, and superintending numerous pet projects for ennobling and raising the standard of social morality amongst the masses. She was not an indifferent mother; she was only an active, busy woman, who, after carefully selecting a thoroughly good and trustworthy woman as her nurse, left the children's training with perfect confidence to her. And between her social and charitable claims there was not much time for having her little ones about her. A young governess came every day for two hours to teach the three eldest ones, but their life was essentially a nursery one. And when the House was closed, and the husband and wife would go off to the Continent or to the Highlands, the children would be sent to a quiet seaside town with their nurse and the nursery maid.

The following afternoon a little figure stole quietly down to the library door. Betty knew her father was out, and Mr. Roper never repulsed any of the children. After a timid knock she passed in, and made a little picture as she stood in the firelight, in her brown velveteen frock and large white-frilled pinafore.

'Well,' said Mr. Roper, wheeling round from his writing-desk, 'what do you want, Betty?'

'I want one of father's books,' the child said earnestly, 'one that Dick Somebody wrote—a book that tells the meaning of everything.'

'I wish there was such a one in existence,' said the young man, smiling a little sadly. 'Now what is in your little head, I wonder?'

'It's a word I want to find, please.'

'Oh, a word! Bless the child, she means a dictionary!' and Mr. Roper laughed as he drew a fat volume out of a shelf, and placed it on a table by the little girl.

'May I help you to find it?'

'It's tribulation. I don't know how it's spelt.'

He did not ask questions; that was one thing that attracted Betty towards him. She was a curious mixture of frankness and reserve. She would confide freely of her own free will, but if pressed by questions would relapse at once into silence. He found the word for her, and she read with difficulty, 'Trouble, distress, great affliction.'

'Do they all mean tribulation?' she asked.

'Tribulation means all of them,' was the answer.

'And can children have tribulation, Mr. Roper?'

'What do you think?'

'I must have it if I'm to get to heaven,' she said emphatically; and then she left him, and the young man repeated her words to himself with a sigh and a smile, as he replaced the book in its resting-place.

CHAPTER II

'MOTHER NATURE'

A few evenings after this, as nurse was undressing the little girls for bed, Mrs. Stuart came into the nursery. She was going out to dinner, and looked very beautiful in her soft satin dress and pearls. She was tall and stately, with the same golden hair as Molly, but her face was somewhat cold in expression.

Sitting down in an easy chair by the fire she asked,—

'What is the matter with Betty? is she in disgrace again?'

Betty was standing in her long nightdress at the foot of her small bed; her hands were clenched, and there was a resolute, determined look upon her flushed face.

'One of her obstinate fits,' said nurse angrily; 'she generally goes to bed before Miss Molly, and because I have let her stay up a little later to-night she is as contrary as she can be! I can do nothing with her, a good whipping is what she wants!'

Betty's blue eyes wandered from nurse's face to her mother's, as if seeking consolation there; her hands relaxed, and a slight quiver came to the little lips.

'Are you going to a party, mother? may I come and kiss you?'

It was Molly who spoke. She was in the act of scrambling into bed, but upon receiving permission she made her way, a little shyly, across to where her mother was seated.

'Now keep your hands off my dress,' Mrs. Stuart said with a smile; but she put her arm round the little figure and kissed her, and sent her back to bed perfectly happy. All the children adored their mother, though it was adoration at a distance.

'Now come here, Betty; what have you been doing? How is it that I never visit the nursery without hearing complaints of your naughtiness?'

'I'm going to be good now,' said Betty, hanging her head, and coming slowly forward into the firelight.

'She has refused to say her prayers,' said nurse sternly.

'I will say them now'; and Betty raised her eyes to her mother somewhat wistfully.

'Why did you refuse to say them when nurse told you to?'

'Because Molly was saying her prayers.'

'Well, what had that to do with it?'

Betty did not answer.

'Answer me.'

The child looked round; nurse had left the room. She worked her little foot backwards and forwards in the long-haired rug rather nervously, and then, almost in a whisper, said,—

'God couldn't listen to both of us, and I wanted Him to listen to me.'

Mrs. Stuart gazed perplexedly at her little daughter, then laughed.

'You are a little goose! Go and say your prayers at once, and get into bed. I have come here to talk to nurse.'

Betty crept away. Her mother's amused laugh had hurt her more than nurse's scoldings. It was hard to have one's secret feelings brought to light and scoffed at, and her sensitive little soul felt this, though in a dim, uncertain way.

'I want to have God all to myself,' was her thought, as a few minutes later she laid her little head down on the pillow; 'I wonder if I'm very wicked. I won't say my prayers if He is not listening.'

'Now, nurse,' said Mrs. Stuart, as that worthy reappeared, 'I want to talk to you. Your master and I are going abroad after Easter; he is not well, and the doctors have ordered him away. I want to send you and the children into the country for the summer. I don't fancy them being at the seaside all that time. You were telling me some time ago of your old home; isn't it a brother of yours who has the farm? Yes? Well, do you think they have room to take you all in?'

Nurse's face glowed with pleasure.

'He has no chick or child, ma'am, and the house is large and roomy; his wife was saying in a letter to me they should like lodgers in the summer. I'm sure it would please them to take us in; and the country round there is wonderfully healthy.'

'I think that would answer very well,' Mrs. Stuart went on thoughtfully; 'we may be away six months: and the children are looking pale, a country life will do them all the good in the world. Let them run wild, nurse, they will come back to their lessons all the better for it. Miss Grant told me this morning she would have to give up teaching—her mother is very ill—so, all things combined, I think this plan will work well. Will you write to your brother and find out if he can take you in the last week in April? Let me know when you have heard from him.'

Mrs. Stuart rose as she spoke; her visits were never long, and nurse left the room with her.

'Betty,' said Molly, in an eager tone, 'did you hear? We're going into the country.'

'I heard; and no lessons, and we're to run wild; how lovely!' Betty's curly head bobbed up and down in excitement, then she said persuasively, 'Molly, let you and me keep it a secret together; we won't tell Douglas or the twins.'

This required consideration. Molly sat up in bed and looked thoughtful.

'I never do have a secret with you,' pleaded Betty. 'You and Douglas have lots; I never have any one to have secrets with.'

'Well, I'll see,' and there was a little of the elder sister in Molly's tone. 'I'll tell you to-morrow morning. Oh, it will be jolly in the country, won't it? And nurse's home that she tells us about is like our story-books: it's full of calves, and lambs, and horses, and ducks, and chickens, and haymaking, and pigs!'

'And ponds, and apple orchards, and we shall have cream, and honey, and strawberries every day!' continued Betty.

The little girls' voices were raised in their excitement, and they did not notice a door at the end of the room slowly open.

'What a row! Are you telling stories?'

It was Douglas, who slept in a little room off the nursery, and who had been roused by the sound of talking.

'Hush! nurse will hear. Come and sit on my bed,' said Molly, 'and then you will hear all about it.'

'Oh, Molly, it was to be our secret!'

'Douglas won't tell. Besides, nurse is sure to tell us; she knew we were awake and listening.'

Betty gave a little sigh, then joined eagerly in giving her brother the delightful information.

He listened, rumpling up his fair curls, and blinking his blue eyes, which were already heavy with sleep.

'Easter is years off,' he said at last. 'Why, we are still in winter. I daresay we shan't go, after all.'

'We are in February now,' said Molly, looking a little disappointed at the calm way he received such rapturous news.

'If I go,' Douglas went on meditatively, 'I shall ask father to let me have a gun, and I shall shoot rabbits and birds every day.'

'Then you'd be a wicked, cruel boy!' pronounced Betty indignantly. 'I shall catch all the rabbits I can see and tame them.'

'Then I shall let them loose again,' retorted Douglas; and taking up Molly's pillow, he flung it with all his strength at Betty, who instantly returned it, and a pillow fight commenced. Molly joined delightedly in the fray; but, alas! in the height of the excitement, Betty backed into a can of water put ready for their morning bath. Over she went, head first, on the floor, and the whole contents of the can flooded her and the carpet together. Douglas precipitately fled into his little room, and Molly into her bed, so that when nurse came hastily in Betty again was discovered as chief offender. Whilst she was being hustled into a dry nightdress nurse relieved her vexed feelings by giving her a good scolding, and Betty eventually crept into bed wondering if she was really the 'wickedest, mischievousest child on earth,' or if grown-up people sometimes made mistakes.

For the next few days nothing was talked of but the proposed country visit; but as weeks went on, and spring seemed still as far away, the children's excitement subsided, and the ordinary routine of lessons, walks, and play engrossed their whole attention.

But Easter came at last, and then packing-up began. Miss Grant took her departure, and poor Sophy, the nursery maid, had her hands full enough, for nurse's command was to keep the children quiet, and not let them come near her when packing.

Mr. Roper was leaving the library one afternoon about four

o'clock, when he saw the disconsolate little figure of Betty seated on the stairs.

'Anything the matter?' he asked good-naturedly.

'We're going away to-morrow,' was the reply, 'and it is all topsy-turvy upstairs. Douglas and Molly have been lions for hours, and Bobby and Billy two monkeys, and I've been the man. I'm tired of being him, and they won't let me change. I've broken a jug and basin, and nearly pulled a cupboard over, and spilt a bottle of cod-liver oil all over Billy's hair, and upset nurse's work-basket, and then I ran away and hid, and came down here. You don't know how tiring it is to be hunted by four animals all at once.'

Mr. Roper sat down on the stairs by her and laughed heartily. 'Poor little hunter!' he said, 'and how does nurse bear all this raging storm around her?'

'Oh, nurse is with mother, in the night nursery. Sophy is running after all of us. I don't know who she pretends to be, but when I left her she was sitting on the floor wiping Billy's hair and crying.'

Betty's tone and face were grave, and Mr. Roper stopped laughing. 'Have you been thinking over tribulation any more?' he asked.

Betty nodded.

'A lot,' she said emphatically, then shut up her little lips tightly; and Mr. Roper knew he was to be told no more.

'Are you going into the country, Mr. Roper?' he was asked presently.

'No, indeed. I am not rich enough to have such a holiday as is in prospect for you. I wonder what you will do with yourselves all the time? You must come back much the better and wiser, Betty, for it.'

'Why?'

'You will be six months older, and old Mother Nature is the best governess for little ones like you. She will teach you many a lesson, if you keep your eyes and ears open.'

Betty's eyes were very wide open now.

'Does she live at the farm? I never heard nurse speak of her. We don't want another governess there. How do you know her?'

'I knew her when I was a little boy, and loved her. I love her now, but my work is in London, and I never get much chance of seeing her.'

'She must be very old,' Betty said meditatively.

'Very old; and yet every year she seems younger and more beautiful. You will see her at her best, Betty. I shall expect you to come home and tell me all about her.'

'Shall I give her your love and a kiss when I see her?'

'Yes,' said the young man, smiling down upon the earnest child beside him.

A rush of feet behind them, and Molly and Douglas came tearing downstairs.

'Here she is! Where have you been? Bobby has cut his head

open, and Sophy has rushed to nurse, and nurse is scolding away, so we came off. Mr. Roper, do you know we're going away to-morrow?'

'And will you come and see us one day, Mr. Roper?'

'Mr. Roper, does every farmer in the country go about in his night-shirt? Douglas says they do, and we have pictures of them.'

'And are there stags and wild boar to hunt? Do tell us.'

Mr. Roper made short work of these questions, and departed. He was a reserved, reticent man, and did not understand the boisterous spirits of the little Stuarts. Betty was his favourite; he was always ready for a chat with her, but the others worried him.

Nurse was very thankful when she got herself and her little charges all comfortably settled in the railway carriage for Tiverstoke the next day. Sophy was not going with them, but the longing to be in the old home again quite compensated nurse for the additional labour and responsibility she would have.

The children had parted from their parents with great composure. Mrs. Stuart had reiterated parting injunctions to nurse, and their father had presented all five with a bright half-crown each, which gift greatly added to their delight at going.

'Not much affection in children's hearts,' said Mr. Stuart to his wife, as he watched the beaming faces gathered round the cab window to wave 'good-bye.'

'They will get through life the better for absence of sentiment and demonstrativeness,' replied Mrs. Stuart; and perhaps those words were an index to her character.

CHAPTER III

WAS IT AN ANGEL?

It was a lovely afternoon in May, a week after the children's arrival at Brook Farm. They were together in the orchard, which was a mass of pink and white bloom. Bobby and Billy were having a see-saw on a low apple branch; Douglas was perched on a higher bough of a cherry tree, and the little girls were lying on the ground. Tongues were busy, as usual.

'We've seen everything round the house,' Douglas was asserting in rather a dictatorial tone; 'and now we must be busy having adventures—people always do in the country.'

'What kind?' asked Molly meekly.

'They get tossed by bulls, or lost in the woods, or drowned in ponds,' Douglas went on thoughtfully.

'I'm not going to do any of those.'

And Betty's tone was very determined.

'What are you going to do, then?'

'I shall be busy all by myself. I'm going out to look for

some one.'

'Who?' asked Molly curiously.

'Some one Mr. Roper told me about. He sent his love to her and a kiss. It's a secret between me and Mr. Roper, I shan't tell you any more.'

And Betty rolled over in the grass with a delighted chuckle at the puzzled faces round her.

'It's only one of her make-ups,' Douglas said, recovering his composure. 'Let me tell you of my plans. Do you see those thick trees at the top of that hill? That's a real wood. Now, if nurse sends us out tomorrow afternoon while she takes a nap, I'm going there, and you girls must come after me.'

'And us, too,' put in Bobby, listening attentively.

'If you can walk so far, and don't go telling nurse about it.'

'How far is it? Six miles?' asked Molly, who would have been willing to walk ten, had her brother so ordained.

'It is only through three fields, Sam told me.'

Sam was one of the carters, who had already become one of Douglas's greatest friends.

'He be the pluckiest, knowingest little chap that ever oi see wi' such a baby face!' was the carter's opinion of him.

'If it's a very nice wood perhaps I'll come,' said Betty.

'You must save something from dinner to take with us, for we will have a feast when we get there.'

This sounded delightful, and all spent the rest of the day in busy confabulation as to how they could get there without being stopped by any one, and what provisions they must take.

But, alas! when the next day came, nurse announced her intention of taking Douglas and Molly with her to tea with a friend, a little distance off, and so the visit to the wood was postponed.

Betty pleaded to be allowed to go with them, but nurse refused.

'I can't have more than two; and I'm taking them more to keep them out of mischief than anything. Mrs. Giles is going to look after the little ones, so you must amuse yourself.'

Betty felt rather disconsolate after they had gone. She wandered into the farm kitchen, where Mrs. Giles, a good-natured, smiling woman, was busy making bread. The twins were in a corner playing with some kittens. Betty stood at the table watching. At last she looked up a little shyly and said,—

'Mrs. Giles, do you know a very nice governess that lives here?'

'A guviness, bless your little heart. There's Miss Tyler in the village, two mile off—but I don't think much of her. She's too giddy and smart, and the way she carries on with Dan Somers is the talk of the place! Are you after having lessons then?'

'Oh no, no, no!' cried Betty eagerly, 'that's why I don't talk about it to any one; but I should like to see her, for I have a message to give her. I don't think it can be Miss Tyler;

Mother Nestor—I forget the name, but something like Nestor or Nasher—Mr. Roper called her. She's old and young together, and very pretty.'

Mrs. Giles laughed. 'Old and young together! I know of nought like that; when we gets old, youth don't stick to us. Do you think I answer to that description, Miss Betty?'

'I should say you were very old,' observed Betty reflectively, 'not a bit young; but I think your red cheeks are very pretty.'

Mrs. Giles laughed again, and Betty left the kitchen saying, 'I'll go out of doors and look for her; perhaps she'll be coming along the road.'

Into the bright sunshine she went, across a clover field, and out at a gate into the white, dusty road. She trotted along, picking flowers by the wayside, and peeping over hedges to look at the tiny lambs or young foals and heifers sporting on the green grass. Everything was new and delightful to her; the birds singing, the budding trees, the bright blue sky, and sweet fresh air, all was filling her little heart with content and happiness. Wandering on, she kept no reckoning of time or distance, until she came to a church in the midst of green elms, and rooks keeping up a perpetual chatteration on the topmost branches of the trees.

Betty was a little afraid of rooks; they were so big and strong and black that she feared they would peck her legs; but she was very tired and warm, and as the church-gate was open she thought she would venture into the cool shade of the elms inside. Her little steps took her to the church porch, and finding the door partly open, with a child's curiosity, she pushed her way in, there to stand with admiring awe in the cool, quiet atmosphere. It was a pretty old church, with stained glass windows; and the sun streaming through sent flashing rays of red and blue, golden and purple, across the old stone walls and oaken seats.

Betty felt she was in another world at once, and the very novelty and strangeness of her surroundings had a great charm for her. Slowly she made her way round the church, looking at every tablet and monument, and trying in vain to decipher the writing upon them. But one amongst them brought her to a standstill: it was the figure of a little girl sculptured in white marble, lying in a recumbent position; her hands were crossed on her breast, with a lily placed between them, her eyes were closed, and her hair curled over her brow and round her shoulders in the most natural way. Just above her was a stained glass window—a beautiful representation of the Saviour taking the children in His arms and blessing them. Below the window was written in plain black letters,—

IN LOVING MEMORY OF VIOLET RUSSELL.

Aged six years.

'Suffer the little children to come unto Me, and forbid them not.'

Betty drew a deep breath; her thoughts were busy. She wished herself that little girl lying so calm and beautiful, with the red and golden rays slanting across her; and then looking up at the window, she wished still more that she was one of those happy children in the Lord's arms.

Looking up with tearful eyes, she clasped her hands, and let her buttercups and bluebells fall to the ground unheeded.

'O God, I will be good! I will be good!'

Those were all the words uttered, but He who heard them looked down into the overflowing heart, and knew all that lay behind them.

Long the child stood there, and then with flagging footsteps made her way down the aisle.

'I'm very tired,' she murmured to herself; 'I'll just sit down inside that pew.'

And a moment after, curling herself up on the cushions, Betty went fast asleep.

She was dreaming soon of a wonderful white-robed throng; she saw the little girl walk up with her white, still face to a golden throne, she tried to follow, but could not manage to walk, and then the most wonderful music began to sound; louder and clearer it came, until with a start she opened her eyes and discovered where she was. Was it all a dream? The music was still sounding in her ears, and sitting up she peered over the edge of the high pew. There, seated at the organ, was a lady, and she was pouring forth such a flood of melody and song that it did indeed seem to the half-wakened child music straight from heaven.

Betty listened breathlessly to the words—words that she knew now so well, and that were ever in her thoughts: 'These are they which came out of great tribulation, and have washed their robes and made them white in the blood of the Lamb.'

It was a beautiful anthem, and a beautiful voice that was singing. Betty had never heard such singing before. She gazed with open mouth and eyes; the lady was rather a young one, she noticed, and when her voice rose in triumph and the organ pealed out in accompaniment, Betty saw that her uplifted eyes, shining as they were with such a glad light behind them, were full of tears.

'It's an angel,' she whispered to herself. And when at last the notes died away, and there was stillness in the church, when she saw the lady's face bowed in her hands, as if in prayer, Betty stole softly out of the building, and retraced her steps along the road, sobbing as she went. It had been too much for her excitable little brain; she always had been passionately fond of music, but was more accustomed to the street organs in London than to any other sort, and this was as great a contrast to those as heaven is to earth.

It was a long way back, but Betty did not feel it. Had God sent an angel to sing to her? Was there a chance of her ever being amongst that white-robed throng? If she could only go through tribulation! Had the little girl lying so white and still gone through it? These and other similar puzzling thoughts came crowding through her brain.

She was very quiet when she reached the farm. They were just sitting down to tea when she came in, and Mrs. Giles looked relieved when she saw her.

'We was wonderin' where you had got to,' she said. 'Ain't you tired? You look quite beat.'

'I've had a lovely afternoon,' was the child's answer, and the blue eyes shone up at her questioner; but not a word more could be got from her, though the little boys did their best to extract more information.

The next day was a wet one, but the little Stuarts were never at a loss for occupation, and when they were packed off into a large empty garret for the whole afternoon their delight was unbounded.

Amy Le Feuvre

At last, tired out, their spirits began to flag, and after having exhausted all their stock of games they flung themselves down on the ground to rest.

'I'll tell you a story,' said Betty suddenly.

'All right, go on!'

Betty sat up in a corner, and rested her back against the wall. She clasped her small hands in front of her, and gazing dreamily up at an old beam across the room, on which hung many a cobweb, she began,—

'It was a beautiful day in heaven—'

'It's always a beautiful day there,' put in Douglas critically.

'I never said it wasn't. You're not to interrupt me. It was a beautiful day, the harps were playing and the angels singing, and one angel looked as if she wanted something. So God asked her what was the matter.

'"Oh, please," she said, "I want to go down to earth to-day."

'"What do you want to do there, O angel?"

'"I want to play and sing to some children there."

'Then God said she might go. So she flew down and changed her clothes—'

'What kind of clothes did she put on?' asked Molly eagerly.

Betty considered a moment 'She put on a straw hat and a grey dress; she took off her wings and folded them up.'

'Where did she put them?' demanded Douglas.

'Down a well,' was the prompt reply. 'It was a dry well, and she put her white dress and crown with it; she did them up in a paper parcel, and wrote her name on.'

'What was her name?' asked Bobby.

Betty knitted her brows. 'It was a Bible name, of course; I think it was Miriam. She felt the earth was very hot, for the sun was shining like anything, and then she wondered who she could sing to. Well, she walked along a road, and then she saw a church, so she thought that must be a good place, and she went inside. The church was dark, and cool, and still, but it was lovely; and there were red and blue and yellow and green and violet sunbeams, and beautiful painted windows, and white marble figures all about, and it was so still that you felt you must hush and walk on tiptoe. And then, what do you think she saw?'

All eyes were on Betty now, as she sank her voice to an impressive whisper.

'She saw a little girl fast asleep!'

'Go on,' said Douglas impatiently, as Betty made another pause.

'So the angel thought she would sing to her; so she went up very softly to the big organ, and began to play it, and then she began to sing. It was lovely. She sang like she did in heaven, and the little girl woke up and listened.'

'What did she sing about?' asked Molly.

'She sang about heaven, and all the people and children who

had come through great tribulation. And the music went on right up to the top of the church, and her voice got louder and louder, and then softer and softer to a whisper, and then the music got softer too, and then—it was quite still.'

'Well, go on. What did the little girl do?'

'The little girl came away; she—she cried a little.'

'Why, you're crying too! What a silly!'

Betty dashed her small hand across her eyes, and threw up her head defiantly. 'That's all my story,' she said.

'Oh, what a stupid story! You must make a proper ending.'

'You shall go on! we'll make you!'

'Did the angel get her proper clothes again?'

'Yes,' said Betty, with a little sigh; 'she put them on and went up to heaven. And God asked her what she'd done. And she told Him she thought the little girl would like to come to heaven, if He would let her.'

There was a little break in Betty's voice; she slid down from her corner, and rolled over on the floor, her face hidden from the others. Then in a second she called out, 'I see a mouse! Let us catch him!'

The children were on their feet directly, and a regular scramble ensued, Betty the most boisterous of them all. And when nurse came in a little later, she found the little story-teller in the act of crawling across the oaken beam in the centre of the room, to the intense delight of those watching her below.

Nurse caught her breath at the daring feat, but waited till she had accomplished it in safety, then caught her in her arms, and taking her off, gave her a good whipping, and Betty's spirits totally subsided for the rest of the evening.

CHAPTER IV

ADVENTURES

The visit to the wood came off the day after. Nurse arrayed all her little charges in large holland overalls, and sent them out into the fields for the afternoon. And the little party set out in good spirits, Bobby and Billy tramping sturdily along, under the firm conviction that they were going to meet with wild beasts, and go through the most harrowing adventures.

It was a long walk, but they reached it at last, and came to a standstill when they saw the ditch and the thick hedge that surrounded it.

'There's a castle and a princess inside, so they don't like people to come in,' asserted Douglas; 'but we'll find a hole somewhere and creep through.'

And this was soon done. The children looked round them with delight at the little winding paths, the banks of green moss, and the thick overhanging bushes and trees, that seemed so full of life and interest. Douglas was in his element.

'We'll find a place we must call home first, and then we'll see what food we've got.'

The foot of an old oak tree was chosen. Bits of cake, pudding, some biscuits, and a few lumps of sugar were then produced from different pockets, and these were given over to Douglas, who, wrapping them in paper, deposited them inside the hollow trunk of the tree.

'Now,' he said, 'we must all divide, and go in search for adventures; and when we've found them, we can come back and tell the others here, and then we'll have a feast.'

'And if we don't find any?' questioned Betty doubtfully.

'Then you must go on till you do. Why, of course a wood is full of dangers. I mean to have an *awful* time. We must go two and two; Molly and I will take this path, and the twins can take that one, and you, Betty, must go by yourself, because you're the odd one.'

'I always have to go alone,' murmured Betty; 'it isn't fair.'

Bobby and Billy stood clasping each other's hands, and looking with anxious though determined faces along the path mapped out for them.

'And if we should meet a cwocodile?' Billy asked, lifting his blue eyes to those of his big brother.

'Then you must either kill it or run away,' said Douglas. 'And crocodiles don't live in woods.'

'And if we lose ourselves in the wood?' questioned Bobby.

'If you're frightened, you needn't go, but stay here till we come back,' put in Molly, her conscience a little uneasy with turning such little fellows loose on their own resources.

But this gave the twins courage. Frightened! Not a bit of it! And they trotted off, calling out they were going to kill every one they met.

Betty likewise started on her journey. She was feeling rather depressed with the truth of which she was always being reminded—namely, that she was the odd one.

'I wish there had just been one more of us,' she kept saying to herself; 'I'm either one too many or one too few, and it's very dull to be always alone.'

But her thoughts soon left herself when she saw some rabbits scudding away in the distance; and the flowers on her path, and the strangeness of her surroundings, were quite enough to occupy her mind. She soon found that her path was coming to an end; right across it was some fine wire netting, and for a moment she hesitated, then, deciding to go straight on, clambered over it with great difficulty. The grass was smoother here, and the path a wide one; a little distance farther was an iron seat, and then she came to a long, straight grass walk, with trees on either side, and at the end a gate, in an old stone wall.

'I shall have to get through that gate,' she mused, 'or else I must climb the wall. I wonder what is inside! It might be anything—a castle, with an ogre or giant, or a prince and princess—and I can't go back till I find out. My adventures have come. But I'm very tired. I'll just sit down for a little before I go on.'

A few moments after Betty's little body was lying full length on the grassy path, and she was counting over a cluster of primroses with great care and precision.

'Twenty-one, twenty-two, twenty-three—ah, what a pity!

there is a little odd one, just like me!'

'What are you doing, child?'

Betty started to her feet. Looking down upon her was a tall old lady, dressed in a shady straw hat and black lace shawl; her black silk dress rustled as she moved. One hand was resting on a stick, the other was holding a sunshade. Her face was as still and cold-looking as some of the figures on the monuments in the little village church, and her voice stern and peremptory.

Wild thoughts flashed through Betty's brain. Was this a fairy godmother, a queen, a princess? Or might it possibly be the old governess that Mr. Roper loved so much?

Again the question was repeated, in the same stern tone, and Betty gazed up in awe, as she answered simply,—

'I was counting the primroses, to see if they were even or odd.'

'And what business have you to be trespassing in my private grounds?'

'I didn't know this was trespassing,' Betty faltered; 'a wood belongs to anybody in the country, and I haven't got inside your gate yet, though I was going to try.'

'And pray what were you coming inside my gate to do?'

'I'm—I'm looking for adventures; I have to do something before I go back.'

'I think you had better explain to me who you are.'

The voice was gentler, and Betty took courage. The lady listened to her attentively, and seemed interested; she even smiled when Betty, looking up, asked innocently, 'I suppose you are not a princess, are you?'

'No, I'm not a princess,' she said; 'but this is a private wood, and I cannot allow children to run wild all over it.'

'And mustn't we ever come here again?' asked Betty, with a grave face. 'We should be ever so careful, and we won't pick a flower if you'll only let us walk about. We've never seen a wood before, only read about one in our story-books; and children always go through woods in books without being stopped, unless it's an ogre or a giant that stops them.'

The lady did not speak for a minute, then she said,—

'How many are there of you?'

'Five with me; there's Molly and Douglas, and there's Bobby and Billy—I'm the odd one.'

'Why should you be the odd one?'

'Because Molly and Douglas are the eldest ones, and they always go together, and Bobby and Billy are the babies. Mother always calls them the babies, and I come in between, and I belong to no one. You see, in our games it's generally two and two; I always make everything odd, and Molly and Douglas are always having secrets, and that only leaves me the babies to play with, and they're only just four years old— much too small for me.'

'I suppose you have a doll or something to comfort yourself with? I remember I used to when I was a little girl.'

'I don't much like dolls,' said Betty, with a decided shake of her curly head; 'I like something really alive, something that moves by itself. There's a big sheepdog at our farm called Rough. I sometimes get hold of him for a game, but he likes Douglas better than me. Sam says he's always fond of boys.'

'Would you like to come inside my gate?' asked the lady, looking down upon Betty with a strange tenderness in her eyes, though her lips were still grave and stern.

Betty slipped her hand confidingly into hers.

'Yes, please; and will you tell me who you are? I think you're rather like a lady I'm trying to find. She teaches children, a governess she is, and she's old and young together. You're much more like her than Mrs. Giles is.'

But the lady did not satisfy Betty's curiosity; she only said,—

'I have never taught any children in my life,' and led her up the grassy walk to the gate in the wall.

'I am only going to let you stand inside for a moment, and then you must run away. And you must never come over the wire netting in the wood again. You and your brothers and sister can play in the other part of the wood, but I will not have children running over my private walks.'

She opened the gate, and Betty saw a lovely flower garden, with a smooth, grassy lawn, and away in the distance a great white house. The flowers were exquisite, and to Betty's London eyes they were a feast of delight. Her little face flushed with pleasure.

'Do you live here?' she asked. 'How happy you must be!'

'Do you like it better than my wood?'

Betty turned from the blaze of sunshine and brightness to look at the cool green glade behind her. She did not answer for a minute, then she said, pointing with her small finger down the grassy avenue,—

'It's something like church down there, it looks so quiet. But this garden is like heaven, I think.'

The lady smiled. 'I will give you any flower you like to take away, so choose.'

Betty was not long in making her choice. There were some beautiful white lilies close by—lilies that might have come from the same plant as that one lying between the little girl's hands in church.

'I should like one of those, please,' she said, with sparkling eyes.

She was given, not one, but several, and then was dismissed.

'And I shall never see you again,' Betty said, as she put up her mouth for a kiss. She did not say it regretfully, only as if stating a fact.

The lady stooped and kissed her. 'Not unless I send for you,' she said. 'Can you find your way back?'

Betty nodded brightly, and ran off. The lady stood watching her little figure for some minutes, then she gave a deep sigh, and her face relapsed into its usual stern and immovable expression as she entered her garden and locked the gate behind her.

Betty ran on as fast as she could to join the others. When she reached the oak tree, Douglas and Molly were already there, seated on the ground, busily employed in dividing the provisions for the feast. They exclaimed at the sight of her flowers.

'I've had a lovely adventure,' said Betty. 'Where are Bobby and Billy?'

'We don't know,' said Molly, rising to her feet and looking anxious. 'I'm sure they ought to be here by this time.'

'Perhaps they're lost,' Douglas suggested cheerfully; 'I was hoping some of us would get lost, and then we should have the fun of finding them. We'll go in a few minutes and look for them. Would you like to hear where we have been, Betty?'

'Yes.'

'Well, it is rather a stupid wood, for we came to nothing particular; only we've found a little house. It has three sides and a roof—tumbling in. We're going to mend it up, and live there, next time we come out here. At least, I mean to live in it. I shall be a disguised prince hiding for my life, and you will all have to search the wood to get food for me. Molly and I have made it all up. She is to be my daughter, who steals out at night time to visit me; you can be a servant, who mends the roof, and makes me comfortable; and the twins can be soldiers scouring the wood for me.'

Neither Betty nor Molly showed much interest in this plan; they were both thinking of the twins, and Douglas, having said his say, was quite ready to start off on the quest.

Together they ran along the path by which the little boys had gone. It led them under some low brushwood, and then along the banks of a stream. And then calling their names aloud, they were relieved to hear an answering call. A moment later and they came upon them. The stream was broad, and rather deep here, with great boulders of stone appearing above the water. Upon one of these boulders, in the centre of the stream, sat the two little boys, wet to the skin, and looking the pictures of abject despair.

'However did you get there?' said Douglas rather angrily.

'Billy was getting some forget-me-nots, and tumbled in, and so I came over to help him, and we can't get back,' explained Bobby, not very lucidly.

'If you got over there you can get back again,' Molly said decisively.

At this both the twins began to cry.

'It's so cold; we was nearly drownded; and we've seen a shark swim along.'

Douglas laughed, but took off his shoes and stockings.

'I shall have to wade in and bring them over on my back,' he said, with rather a lordly air.

And this he did, landing both the twins safely on the bank.

'Nurse will scold awfully, they're both so wet; we shall have to go home at once,' said prudent Molly, as with very small handkerchiefs she and Betty tried to wipe some of the wet off their clothes.

'And then she'll say we're never to come to the wood again. I wish we hadn't brought them with us!'

It was a quiet little party that returned to Brook Farm; and in the excitement of receiving the vials of nurse's wrath, and the fuss made over the poor little victims, Betty's adventures remained still unheard and unknown.

She was not sorry that this was so, and was quite content to muse in the secrecy of her own heart upon the beautiful cold lady who had given her the lilies. She thought of her sleeping and waking, and with a strange longing wondered if she would ever be allowed to see her again.

The next afternoon was a very warm one; but Betty's restless little feet could not stay in the buttercup meadow close to the house, where the others were playing, and soon a small white figure in a large sun-bonnet could have been seen plodding along the dusty road towards the churchyard in the distance.

Her little determined face relaxed into wonderful softness when she entered the cool church. Going on tip-toe up the aisle, she came to the monument of little Violet Russell, and here she paused, then clambering up with a little difficulty, she laid two fresh lilies by the side of the sculptured one, across the clasped hands of the child's figure.

'There,' she said in a hushed voice; 'you shan't always hold a cold dead lily, Violet dear; I've brought them to you from my own self, because they're mine, and I'll get you some other flowers when they are dead.'

She put her soft red lips down and left a kiss on the little clasped hands, and then slipped down to the ground again, where she stood for a moment looking up at the stained window above. A noise startled her: walking up the middle aisle was the lady who had played to her before, and following her a rough country boy, who disappeared through a little door behind the organ.

Betty slipped behind a pillar, and watched eagerly. Yes, she was going to play again; and her heart beat high with expectation. She crept into one of the high, old-fashioned pews, and sitting on a hassock, leant her little head back upon the seat, and prepared herself to listen.

The music began, and sent a little shiver of delight through Betty's soul. The long, soft notes that died away like a summer breeze, the deep, grand rolls that seemed to come from a cavern below, and then blend with the clear, sweet echoes rising and falling, and at length ascending in a burst of praise and gladness—it seemed to her that the angels above would be stooping to listen to such strains.

And then, after a little, the lady began to sing; and Betty drew in one deep breath after another. It must be an angel, surely! and yet there was something in the fresh holland dress and shady hat of the singer this afternoon that seemed hardly suitable for an angel's apparel.

The lady once looked round; and Betty thought her face looked sad; but when she began to sing her face was illumined with such light and gladness that the child watched it entranced.

An hour passed, and then the singer was startled by the sound of a sob. She was singing 'Oh, that I had wings like a dove!' and turning round, was startled at the sight of a white sun-bonnet and two small hands grasping the back of one of the pews. Betty had mounted on the hassock to have a full view of the singer long ago, and was now trying in vain to restrain the pent-up feelings of her sensitive little soul.

In an instant the lady had left her seat and come up to the child.

'What is the matter, little one? How did you find your way in here?' she asked gently, as she put her arm round the sobbing child.

But Betty could not put her feelings into words; she only shook her head and sobbed, 'I like the music; don't stop singing.'

'I must stop now: my hour is up. Tell me who you are.'

Betty made an effort to recover her self-possession.

'I'm only Betty,' she said, dabbing her face with her handkerchief; 'are you an angel?'

'Indeed I am not; do I look like one?'

And the lady threw back her head and laughed in a very amused way.

'Not now,' said Betty soberly; 'but you did look like one when you were singing, and I—I hoped you might be.'

'Why did you hope so?'

Again Betty was silent; then, looking up, she seemed to gather courage from the kind face looking down upon her, and burying her face in the lady's dress, she sobbed out,—

'I thought God might have sent you; and then you could have told me lots of things I wanted to know.'

'Perhaps God may have sent me instead of an angel. Tell me

some of the things you want to know.'

'I want to know about Violet, and heaven, and tribulation,' murmured Betty a little incoherently; and then she started as the church clock in the belfry began to chime five.

'It's tea-time; nurse will be looking for me.'

The lady stooped and kissed her. 'I must go too,' she said; 'will you come and see me to-morrow afternoon? I shall be here at the same time, and then we can have a little talk.'

'What is your name?' asked Betty.

'Nesta,' the young lady answered, a little briefly.

'And do you teach children?' was the next question, breathlessly put.

'Sometimes; on Sundays I do.'

Betty's face lighted up, but she said no more, and trotted out of the church and along the road as hard as ever she could.

CHAPTER V

PRINCE

The children were all at breakfast the next morning in the old-fashioned kitchen. Nurse and her brother were having an animated talk over some reminiscences of the past, when there was a knock at the back door, and Mrs. Giles went out. Coming back, she appeared with a small hamper under her arm, which she placed on the floor.

"Tis the queerest thing I know of,' she said; 'look at the label now, Jack; whoever is it for?'

Every one crowded round at once.

'For the little odd one at Brook Farm.'

"Tis for one of the children,' said Jack, rubbing his head; 'they be the only little 'uns that I know of.'

'It's for Betty!' shouted Douglas and Molly excitedly; 'she's the odd one! Open it quick, Betty; perhaps it's a big cake.'

'It's alive!' exclaimed nurse, as on her knees she tried to undo the fastenings. 'Come along, Miss Betty, you shall open it for yourself.'

Betty came near, and with trembling fingers cut the string.

A minute after, and out of the hamper jumped a beautiful little black and white spaniel.

There were screams of delight from all the children, and great surmises as to who could have sent it. Betty guessed, but said nothing when she found a piece of paper tied to a brass collar round his neck, with these words: 'From a friend, hoping he may prove a true companion.'

She clasped her arms round the dog's neck in ecstasy. 'He is my very, very own,' she said, looking up at nurse with shining eyes; 'and I'll have him for ever and ever.'

The little creature sniffed at her face, and then put out his tongue, and gave her a lick of satisfaction and approval. From that time the two were all in all to each other.

There was a great deal of discussion about him that morning, and Betty had to tell of the strange, stern lady who had spoken to her in the wood.

'I'm sure she sent him,' Betty kept repeating; 'I'm sure she did.'

'It was awfully mean to keep your adventure so secret, said Douglas, looking at the dog very wistfully; 'she must be a fairy godmother living in the wood. I wish she would send me something.'

'Perhaps she is a wicked fairy or witch,' suggested Molly, 'who has turned a prince into a little dog, and we must find a kind of spell to bring him back to a prince again.'

'That's what I'll call him,' said Betty, looking up; 'I'll call him Prince.'

Nurse at first demurred at having such an addition to her family, but Mrs. Giles comforted her with the assurance— 'There, let the little miss enjoy him; she'll soon get tired of him—children always do—and when you go back to London you can leave him behind with us. He's a good breed, that we can see; and Jack will be able to sell him if we don't care about keeping him.'

It was fortunate Betty did not hear this suggestion. Prince was rapidly filling a void in her little heart of which only she perhaps had been dimly conscious. She was a child with strong affections and intense feelings, and a yearning to have some one to love, and to be loved in return. None of the little Stuarts were demonstrative, and few guessed how deeply and passionately the bright and mischievous Betty longed for the sympathy and love that was so rarely shown towards her.

So engrossing was the possession of Prince that the day went by, and tea-time came, before Betty thought of her new friend in the church.

But when tea was over she took Molly into her confidence. 'Molly, do you think I might take Prince for a walk? would he follow me?'

'Where are you going?'

'I'm going to see a lady that I think is the governess Mr. Roper told me about; Nesta, her name is, only I think he called her Mother Nesta. I told you about it one night, don't you remember? she's really very old, but she looks very young, and this one must be her.'

'Where did you find her?'

Amy Le Feuvre

'In a church.'

'Oh!' and Molly's tone was indifferent; 'I don't like people in church. Nurse says she is going to take us to church tomorrow. I hoped she would forget; last Sunday it was too far, she said. And Douglas and I were going to have a beautiful church in the orchard. There's an apple tree just like a pulpit.'

'Molly,' called out Douglas, 'Sam is going down to the river to fish; he says he'll show us where we can fish too; do come on!'

Away ran Molly. The twins were playing in the garden porch, and nurse chatting in the kitchen with her sister-in-law. Betty called Prince, who had been busy with a saucer of scraps, and putting on her straw hat set off along the road to church. Prince was certainly a great charge; he was a dog of an inquiring mind, and his continual rushes into the hedge sides, and long searches after young frogs in the grass, considerably delayed his young mistress's progress.

But at length the church was reached; the evening shadows threw long, weird shapes across the darkened path that led to the porch, the rooks were noisier than usual, and Betty looked anxiously down at Prince.

'You won't bark, dear, will you?' she said stooping and lifting him into her arms; 'because church is a very quiet place, and music is the only noise allowed. I'll take you in to see the prettiest little girl you've ever seen, and she's lying so still. I've brought her some forget-me-nots.'

Prince struggled a little at first, but Betty soothed him and then crept inside.

'I'm afraid I've come too late,' she murmured, as she looked round the silent church and saw no signs of the lady; 'but I'll come another day soon and see her.'

Softly she made her way round to the stained-glass window she loved, but started in astonishment when she saw leaning against the monument a tall, strange gentleman.

He did not see Betty; his brows were knitted and his lips twitching strangely under his heavy dark moustache; with folded arms he stood leaning against the pillar, and looking down upon the fair figure of the recumbent child in front of him. Then he stooped, and taking up one of the fading lilies across the child's hands looked at it wonderingly.

'The picture more lasting than the thing itself,' he muttered; 'it is all that is left us; the fragile productions of nature cannot exist long in this hard, rough world, and yet how I tried to shield her from every blast!'

A slight whine from Prince startled him, and looking round he pulled himself together sternly.

'What are you doing here, little girl?'

Almost the same words that had been said to her in the wood the other day; and Betty began to wonder if she were again on forbidden ground.

'Does the church belong to you?' she asked, standing her ground, and looking up through her long dark lashes rather shyly; 'am I where I oughtn't to be? I came to see that little girl.'

He looked at her.

'What do you know about her?'

'I don't know anything, but I want to know. I love her, and I've brought her some more flowers.'

'Did you put these lilies here?'

'Yes; they're quite dead now, aren't they?'

'Of course they are; this is the place of death.'

Betty did not understand the bitter tone; but she said simply, pointing to the child's figure, 'She isn't really dead, is she? She has gone to sleep. I was thinking, when I was here before, if Jesus would only just walk out of that window and touch her hands with His, she would open her eyes and get up. I should like to see her, wouldn't you? I watched her the other day till I almost thought I saw her move. But she will wake up one day, won't she?'

There was no answer.

Betty slipped her little hand in his. 'Would you give her these forget-me-nots, or lift me up so that I can do it?' She had dropped Prince, who was sniffing suspiciously round the gentleman's heels, and waited anxiously for his reply. He took her in his arms, and held her there whilst she placed the flowers in the position she wished; and then, before she was lifted down, she said softly, 'I think she is really singing up in heaven. I like to believe she is there, but I'm not quite sure. Do you know if she came out of tribulation?'

'Why should she?'

'Because it says, about those in white robes with crowns, "These are they which came out of great tribulation, and have washed their robes, and made them white in the blood of the Lamb." It makes me feel very unhappy sometimes, because I haven't been through tribulation yet, and I shan't be ready to die till I have.'

She was set quickly down upon her feet, and without a word the gentleman left her, striding down the aisle and shutting the church door with a slam that echoed and re-echoed through the silent church.

Betty was startled at his sudden departure; she took up her dog in her arms again, and stood gazing silently up at the window above, through which the setting sun was sending coloured rays in all directions. Then with a little sigh she turned and left the church. Outside the porch was a grey-headed old man, the sexton, who was taking his evening walk amongst the graves.

'Hulloo!' he said, 'be you the one that banged this 'ere door just now? 'Twas enough to scare the owls and bats and all the other beasties from their holes for evermore.'

'No, it wasn't me; it was a gentleman.'

'Ah, was it now? Shouldn't be surprised if I knew who it was! 'Twas Mr. Russell, surely! There's no other gent that favours this 'ere building like him.'

'Is he Violet Russell's father?' questioned Betty eagerly.

The old man nodded. 'Yes, he be that little maid's parent, and he'll never get over her loss. She were the apple of his eye, and when she were took, he were like a man demented. Ah, 'tis the young as well as the old I have to dig for!'

'Does that gentleman live here?' asked Betty.

'Ay, surely, for he be the owner of the whole property

hereabout. But 'tis not money will give comfort; he have had a deal o' trouble. I mind when his father turned him out o' doors for his painting and sich-like persoots. And he went to Italy, and there he taught hisself to be a hartist, and painted and carved a lot o' stone figures, and folks say he made a name for hisself in Lunnon. He were taken back by his father after a bit, and came a-coorting Miss Violet Granger, that lived over at Deemster Hall. But his brother, Mr. Rudolph, cut him out, when he went off to Germany for a spell, and he and Miss Violet runned away together, and when he come back he found his bride stolen. He were terrible cut up, and off he goes to foreign parts again, and never a sight of he did us get till the old squire were dead, and Mr. Rudolph had killed hisself out hunting. Then Mr. Frank comes home agen with a bran-new wife, and we thought as how his life were a mending, and things were looking up. He seemed brighter, too; but lack-a-day, 'twere not ten months afore I had to dig a grave for her, and she left him a two-day-old babe to bring up—and little Miss Violet were the joy of his heart—she were a purty, bright little maid, and were out on her little pony every day wi' her father. She just doated on him, and he were as lovin' as a woman wi' her. Then there come the day when the little maid got a ugly fall from her pony, and all the Lunnon doctors were sent for, but could do no good, and she were in bed a wasting away for nigh a twelve-month, and then she died. 'Twere a mercy, for she'd have been a hunchbacked cripple had she lived; and Mary Foster, what were her maid, said as 'ow she suffered terrible at times. The Lord were marciful in takin' of her. But 'tis not to be wondered at Mr. Frank takin' it sorely. And then he shut hisself up in his painting room, and never comed out of it till he had cut the little maid's figure out in stone, like as you see it in the church. Many's the visitor that I've a taken in to see it; and the ladies, they comes away sheddin' tears at the little dear. He put up the coloured window too, and comes to church reg'lar; but he's hard and cold, like the stones he cut, and 'tis his troubles have spoilt him. I mind he were a bright-faced, bonny lad once, that I used to show birds' nests to in the hedges; but now he passes me wi'out a civil word or look. Ay, it's trouble and toil and tribbylation that is man's lot here below!'

Betty listened to this long harangue breathlessly. Much of it she could not follow, but the old man's closing sentence made her look at him eagerly.

'Do you know about tribulation?' she asked.

'Me know of it! Ay, surely, when I've buried six sons and daughters, and last of all my woife, and dug all their graves mysel', save two, which were Jack in Mericky, which died of yellow fever, and only a packet of letters sent back to us belonging to him, and in them there were a bit o' his mother's grey hair which he had cut off that playful afore he went away; and then there were Rob, that were killed down a coal mine, and we could never get at his body, and he left a widder and three childer, and she were married to one o' his chums afore a twelvemonth past—the unfeeling hussy; but I've washed my hands of the lot. Ay, I've been through troubles and tribbylation, which is our lot in this world, but I've had a many more than most folks.'

'Then you must be quite ready to die?' said Betty, looking at him thoughtfully.

The old man looked at her; then rubbed his head in a puzzled way.

'I'm no so sure about that, little lassie; I've seen scores brought into this churchyard and placed in my graves, but there are toimes when I think o' seeing mysel' let down into a strange grave, and one not cut half so foine as mine, for I'm up to my trade, and none could do it better, and I'm thinkin' if that day will wait till I'm ready for it; well—'twill be a good way off yet!'

Betty knitted her brows in perplexity.

'If you've been through tribulation, you must be very nearly ready for heaven—the Bible says so.'

'Ay, do it? Let's hear, missy; for sure I've had my lot o' woe, and the Lord do be marciful!'

For a second time that afternoon Betty repeated the text that was so occupying her mind and thoughts. The old man listened attentively.

'You see,' said Betty, leaning against an old yew tree and hugging Prince close to her, 'it's the first part that's so difficult to me, but it must be quite easy for you. The end of it fits us all, but the tribulation doesn't fit me.'

'And what be the end of it?' asked the sexton.

'It says, they washed their robes and made them white in the blood of the Lamb.'

'Ay,' said the old man, after a minute's silence, 'and 'tis the end of it don't fit me.'

The child looked up, astonishment coming into her blue eyes.

'But that's very easy,' she said, 'that is coming to Jesus and asking Him to wash our sins away in His blood. I thought everybody did that. I do it every night, because I'm an awful wicked girl. I'm always forgetting to be good.'

Again there was silence; the old man looked away over the hills in the distance. It was just the quietest time in the evening; the birds were already in their nests for the night,—even the rooks had subsided; and the stillness and peace around drew his heart and mind upwards. Betty thought he was looking at the sunset, which was shedding its last golden rays over the misty blue outlines of the hills across the horizon. Presently he drew the cuff of his sleeve across his eyes. 'And who be they that the Book says that of?' he asked.

'Why, it's the people in heaven—every one who dies, I s'pose. I like to think of them there, but I do want dreadfully to join them one day; and I'm afraid sometimes I shall be left out.'

Tears were filling the earnest little eyes, and the curly head bent over Prince to hide them.

'I mind,' said the sexton slowly, 'that my missus, before she died, told me to pray, "Wash me, and I shall be whiter than snow." I expect she knew all about the washing, but I've never done much harm to any one, and I've attended church reg'lar.'

'I wish I was as good as you.' And Betty looked up with emphatic utterance. 'I'm always doing some one harm, and nurse will scold me when I get in for being out so late—I know she will. Good-bye, old man.'

She put Prince down on the ground, and trotted off, and the old sexton looked after her with a shake of his head.

'She be a queer little lass! Ay, I would be glad to have her chance of getting to the Kingdom. But I'll have a look at the old Book, and see what it says about this 'ere washing.'

CHAPTER VI

MADE INTO A COUPLE

The next morning being Sunday, the three elder children were taken to church by nurse. It was a small village congregation; and Betty looked round in vain for her friend Nesta. She saw Mr. Russell standing grim and solitary in his large, old-fashioned pew; and she had a nod from the sexton at the church door. The clergyman's wife and grown-up daughter and a few grandly dressed farmers' wives were the only others who occupied seats of their own. The organ was played by the schoolmaster, and after Nesta's playing it did not seem the same instrument. Betty was quieter than her brother and sister; she could see her stained window and little Violet's figure from where she sat; she could even catch sight of her forget-me-nots—now looking withered and dead; and her thoughts kept her restless little body still. Molly and Douglas did not like church; their fair heads were close together, and occasionally a faint sniggle would cause nurse to look round with stern reproval. But at last the long service was over, and they came out into the fresh, sweet air of a June morning.

Nurse had several friends to talk to in the churchyard, and Molly and Betty walked on soberly in front of her, feeling subdued and a little uncomfortable in their stiff white frocks and best Leghorn hats and feathers.

'Where is Douglas?' whispered Betty.

'Hush! don't let nurse know; he saw a pair of legs through a little hole at the back of the organ, and he's gone to see if it is a robber hiding.'

'Will he fight him if it is?' said Betty, with an awe-struck look; then an expression of relief crossing her face, she said, 'I know; it's a boy that goes in at the back whenever a person plays. I don't know what he does, but I've seen him there before.'

'When did you see him?' asked Molly eagerly.

Betty's private adventures never remained secret for long, and she poured forth a long account of her various visits to the church. Molly was much impressed, but Douglas's return soon turned her thoughts into another channel. He looked flushed and dishevelled, and his white sailor suit was soiled and dusty; but nurse was too busy talking to notice his appearance, and he joined the others with some importance in his tone.

'I've made a discovery,' he said; 'how do you think a church organ is played?'

'Like a piano,' said Molly promptly.

'It isn't, then; you turn a handle like the organs in the street, and a man or boy does all the work behind.'

The little girls looked sceptical, and Betty said, 'I'm sure you don't, then, for we can see the person playing.'

'Well, they're only pretending; I've seen the handle myself, and the boy told me if he didn't pull it up and down the organ wouldn't play. It must be like a kind of duet, perhaps. I expect he makes all the big booming notes, and the squeaky notes are made by the person in front. I've promised him sixpence out of my new half-crown, if he'll let me play instead of him one day; and he says he will.'

'Nurse won't let you play it on Sundays,' said Molly; 'besides, you won't be able to do it properly, and if you made a mistake it would be awful.'

'I shall play it on a week-day, and I'll make the old organ sound, you see if I don't!'

Directly the children reached home, Betty flew to her dog, who had been shut up in the garret whilst they had been at church. Prince was already getting to know his little mistress, and welcomed her back with short happy barks and a great many licks. And Betty poured out all her heart's love for him in the shape of caresses and pats and kisses, whispering in his silken ears many a secret, and hugging him to her breast with a passionate vehemence which astonished and amused those who saw her.

'He is my own, my very own,' she kept repeating; 'and I shall never feel odd no more!'

She did not. It was a new and delightful sensation to be one of a couple. 'Molly and Douglas, Bobby and Billy, and Prince and I,' she would say. No longer was she to trot off alone in some of their games,—Prince was always ready to go with her; if Molly and Douglas were deep in some conspiracy, so could she and Prince be; and the pent-up feelings and thoughts of rather a lonely little heart were poured out to one who listened and sympathised with his soft brown eyes and curly tail, but who never betrayed the confidence reposed in him.

At no time in her life had Betty been so happy as she was now; her little pensive face sparkled with gladness when Prince gambolled by her side; and nurse asserted that the dog kept her out of mischief, and was a very successful addition to their party. It was some days before she visited the church again; but when she did, the organ was sounding, and she found her friend already playing. Rolling Prince up in her large holland overall, until only his little black nose peeped out, Betty crept up close to the player, and stood unnoticed for some minutes. Then Nesta Fairfax turned round and gave the child a pleased smile.

'My little friend again!' she said; 'I have been wondering what has become of you. Have you come for a talk?'

'No, only to listen to the music,' said Betty.

'Then I will go on playing.'

She turned back to the organ, and for some time Betty listened in silence, sitting on a hassock and rocking Prince backwards and forwards, till warm and exhausted with his ineffectual struggles to free himself, he fell asleep in her arms.

At last, when there was a pause in the music, Betty said earnestly,—

'Will you sing again what you did when I thought you were an angel?'

'What was it, I wonder?'

'It was about—"these are they which came out of great tribulation!"'

'Oh yes, I remember.'

And the sweet clear voice rang out through the silent church, and the organ rose and fell to the beautiful words, till Betty could hardly bear it.

'Is it over?' she asked, as the last note died away.

Nesta Fairfax turned her glowing face upon the child.

'You love it as much as I do, you little mite!' she said; 'but you mustn't cry. Do you know where those words come from?'

She put her arms round her, and drew her to rest against her as she spoke,—

'Yes,' said Betty with a nod; 'I know all about them; I've read it sixty hundred times, I think, and I know that verse by heart. I want to ask you about it.'

Nesta waited, and with a little effort Betty said,—

'I want dreadfully to be one of them one day, and I'm afraid I never shall. I was talking to the old man who digs graves, the other day; the first part of the verse doesn't fit me, and the last doesn't fit him—at least he said so. I wonder if both parts fit you.'

Nesta gazed at Betty in a puzzled kind of way; then looked away, for her eyes were filling with tears.

'Perhaps it may,' she said softly; 'I should like to think it did.'

'And can you tell me how I can go through tribulation? I want to get it over, so that I can be quite ready for heaven.'

'My dear child, if God means you to have it, He will send it in His own good time. Never wish for troubles; they will come fast enough as you grow older.'

'That's what nurse says; she tells us when we get to her age we shall know what distress and trouble is. But s'posing if I don't live to grow up? Violet didn't, and I'm so afraid I may not get inside heaven. I may be left out of those in the text, because I haven't been through tribulation. I don't want to be left out; I want to be in the very middle of them all! I want to stand singing, and have a crown and a palm, and I want to hear some one ask who I am; and then I want to hear the answer, "She came out of tribulation!" Oh! do tell me how I can go into it! Mr. Roper said you would teach me a lot of things.'

Betty's voice was eloquent in her beseeching tone, and Nesta was silent for a moment; then she said,—

'Trouble doesn't take us to heaven; tribulation, even martyrdom, does not. Don't you know what does? What did Jesus Christ come into the world for? What did He die for? Will you sing a little hymn with me? I expect you know it.'

Betty looked delighted.

'And will you play the organ?'

'Yes.'

Then Nesta began to sing; and Betty's sweet little voice chimed in; for well she knew the words,—

'There is a green hill far away,
Beyond the city wall,
Where our dear Lord was crucified,
Who died to save us all.

We may not know, we cannot tell
What pains He had to bear;
But we believe it was for us
He hung and suffered there.

He died that we may be forgiven,
He died to make us good,
That we might go at last to heaven,
Saved by His precious blood.

There was no other good enough
To pay the price of sin;
He only could unlock the gate
Of heaven and let us in.

Oh, dearly, dearly has He loved,
And we must love Him too,
And trust in His redeeming blood,
And try His works to do.'

'Now can you tell me why the Lord Jesus Christ died; what does the hymn say?'

'He died that we may be forgiven, He died to make us good,' quoted Betty slowly.

'Go on.'

'That we might go at last to heaven, saved by His precious blood.'

'Then how can we get to heaven?'

'Because Jesus died for us.'

'Yes, He died to let you go to heaven, Betty; He did it all, and you have nothing to do with it. If you let Jesus take your little heart and wash it in His blood, nothing will ever keep you out of heaven.'

'But if I'm naughty?' asked Betty. 'I've asked God so often to give me a new heart and wash me in Jesus' blood, and sometimes I think He has done it; but then I'm always getting into mischief, and nurse says it's only the good children go to heaven.'

'I think Jesus will teach you to be good, if you ask Him, and you mustn't expect to be quite good all at once; always go to Him when you've been naughty, and tell Him about it, and ask Him to help you to be good. He loves you, Betty, and He will always listen to you and answer your prayers.'

Betty's blue eyes were looking intently at the speaker; and her little lips took a resolute curve.

'I will be good,' she said; 'I do love Jesus, and I'll ask Him all day long to keep me from being naughty.'

Then after a pause she said,—

'Have you gone through tribulation?'

'I have had a great deal of trouble.' And a sad look came over Nesta's face.

'My old man said he had had a lot of trouble, and he told me Mr. Russell had. Trouble always means people dying, doesn't it?'

'There are troubles worse than death,' Nesta said gravely; 'God grant you may never know such!' Then with a change of tone she said brightly, 'Don't look for trouble, darling; Jesus means you to be happy. Now shall we sing one more hymn, and then I must go.'

Betty joined in delightedly when Nesta began,—

'There's a Friend for little children.'

After it was finished Nesta asked,—

'What did you mean, Betty, by saying that a Mr. Roper had told you I would teach you? Who is Mr. Roper?'

Betty told her, repeating as much of the conversation she had had with him as she could remember; and Nesta laughed aloud when she discovered the origin of the 'lady who taught.'

'He meant Mother Nature, Betty; a very different teacher to me.'

'Do you know her, then? Where does she live?'

'I will take you to see her when next we meet. You see her every day, Betty. Now I must go. Good-bye. Is this a little doggie you have rolled up in your pinafore? I thought it was a doll. Now, Dick, you can come out.'

Dick Green, a heavy-looking village boy, appeared from behind the organ, and followed Miss Fairfax down the aisle. But Betty waited; she had brought two roses with her for Violet's monument, and she went to the seat upon which she had laid them, and took them round to the other side of the church, where she deposited them in the usual place. Then calling Prince, who had been awakened from his sleep, and was now inspecting every corner of the church with nose and paws, Betty set off homewards.

Nesta Fairfax had comforted her, but had not entirely satisfied her perplexed little heart, and the busy brain was still trying to solve the problem.

Betty was not the only visitor to the church that day.

Douglas disappeared after tea, and after nearly two hours' absence returned, hot, tired, and very cross.

At last he confided to Molly that he had been to play the organ.

'And I'm awfully afraid I've broken the horrid old thing, and I don't like that Dick Green! He took my sixpence and ran off, and I worked the handle up and down for hours; he told me the music would come in about a quarter of an hour. It never did, but the organ gave great gasps and groans; you never heard such a noise, just like Mr. Giles when he goes to sleep after tea! It's awfully hard work pulling the handle up and down; I hope I haven't broke it. I think it wants some one to play on the front of it, but the front part is locked up. But I've had a kind of adventure. When I came out there was a strange gentleman looking at one of the graves in the church, so I went up to see what he was looking at, and it was the stone image of a little girl, and there were some pink roses in her hands.'

Betty edged up close to her brother as he got thus far, and asked eagerly, 'What did he say about the roses?'

Amy Le Feuvre

'He looked at me with an awful frown, and I folded my arms and frowned back, like this!'

And Douglas rumpled his fair brow into many creases, and looked so ferocious that Molly was quite awed, though disrespectful Betty laughed aloud.

'"What are you doing here?" he said. "Did you put these roses here?"'

'"No," I said; "oughtn't they to be there? I'll take them away." And then he frowned worse than ever, and said, "Don't you dare to lay a finger on them!" and then he muttered something about the church being always full of children now. But I didn't listen to him much; I was busy looking at the little girl, and thinking, and then I made up a beautiful story on the spot; it's something like some of the fairy stories we read in our big books. I'll tell it to you in a minute. I said to him that I thought I could tell him where the roses came from, and he said "Where?" and then I said to him that the little girl was a sleeping beauty waiting for a prince to come along and kiss her and wake her up; but he hadn't come yet, so a fairy was watching her till he came; and every moonlight night she would bring some flowers in, and creep inside them and sleep with her, to keep all the goblins off, and she would sing her songs in the night, and tell her stories, and comfort her—'

'But,' interrupted Molly, 'if she was asleep, how could she hear the fairy?'

'You're too sharp! Perhaps you'll wait. I was just going to say that in the night she was able to open her eyes, only she couldn't get up. I had just got as far as that, when the gentleman said "Pshaw!" and then he told me to run off, and not come into the church again to tomfool—that's what he said. He was a kind of dark, grim-looking ogre, and I'll—well, I shall have more to do with him yet!'

This awful threat was accompanied with a very significant shake of the flaxen head, but Betty cried out hotly,—

'You don't know anything about it! He's the father of that little girl, and he goes to her grave to say his prayers and cry. I know more about him than you do, so there!'

'What do you know?'

But Betty walked off, hugging Prince under her arm, and calling out as she went, with a spice of superiority in her tone, 'Prince and I know all about him, and her, and the roses; that's *our* secret.'

CHAPTER VII

HAYMAKING

It was only a few days after this that nurse took all the children to tea at an old farmhouse about two miles off. They rode part of the way in a farm waggon, and were all in the best of spirits, for it was haymaking time,—a time of entrancing joy to all children, and to the little Stuarts a new and delightful experience. They had tea out in one of the fields under a shady elm, and were just separating after it was over to have one more romp in the hay, when, to Betty's intense surprise, who should come across the field but Nesta Fairfax! She evidently knew Mrs. Crump, the farmer's wife, well, for she sat down and began chatting away about all her family, and then she caught sight of Betty.

'Why, it's my little friend!' she said, stooping down and kissing her; 'and are these your brothers and sisters?'

Betty got crimson with delight, and introduced one after the other with great importance, and Nesta won all their hearts at once by joining them in their frolic. Her laugh was as gay as theirs, and she could run as fast as any of them.

'You're rather a nice grown-up person,' said Douglas approvingly, as at last she took her leave; 'you aren't so dull and stupid as grown-up people generally are! Will you come and see us one day at our farm? I'll take you to see the sweetest white mice in the stable that Sam keeps, and there's heaps of easy trees to climb in the orchard, if you like climbing!'

'And I'll show you a baby calf only two days old,' put in Molly, 'and three black and white kittens in a loft, with a lot of apples one end. We've jolly things at our farm, if you'll only come.'

'And a see-saw and a swing,' added the twins.

'And what will Betty show me?' asked Nesta, amused.

'I think I'll show you the flowers, and the forget-me-nots and watercress in the brook,' said Betty meditatively.

'Then I really must come, with such an enchanting programme before me,' said Nesta; and she kissed them all round, told nurse she envied her her little family, cracked some jokes with old Crump and his wife, and departed, leaving behind her a breezy brightness and cheeriness that she brought with her wherever she came.

'A pleasant young lady,' said nurse; 'who is she, Mrs. Crump?'

'Ah, well,' said Mrs. Crump, shaking her head solemnly; 'there's a sad story attached to the family. My niece, what the master and I have brought up like one of our own children, has got the sitivation as maid to Mrs. Fairfax, and she knows all the ins and outs of their trouble as no one else do. You see, this is how it is! They were a Lunnon family, and come down here first for change of air. They took lodgings in Mrs. Twist's farm; there were Mrs. Fairfax and the two young ladies, and a dashing young gentleman, the son, who came down for a day or two at a time, but he never stayed long. Mrs. Fairfax were proud as proud could be, and very cold and stern-like except to her son, so Jane says, and him she couldn't do enough for; her heart was just bound up in him! Jane went back with them to Lunnon, but she says the way the young gentleman went on were enough to break any mother's heart. He was fast going to the bad; and yet his mother, though she would scold and fume at times, never seemed to see it, and paid his debts, and let him have his fling. Miss Nesta were engaged to be married, and Jane says her lover did all he could to stand by her brother and keep him straight; but it weren't no good whatever. And about two year ago the end came. Mr. Arthur had some trouble over a gaming-table; that was the beginning; then he went and signed a bank cheque that wasn't his—I believe as how it is called forging, and the gentleman whose cheque it was had him up in court; he wouldn't hush it up, and it was the talk of all Lunnon, so Jane tells me. His mother would have paid up, though it would have ruined her; but she weren't allowed, and he were sent to prison across the seas for seventeen years. Jane says Mrs. Fairfax seemed turned to stone; she shut up the Lunnon house, and went abroad to some foreign place with a long name, I forgets it now; and then she comes back and takes Holly Grange, which is as nice an old house as ever you see, and belonged to a Colonel Sparks, who died only a twelvemonth ago, and is about a mile from here, over against that wood you see yonder. But I'm tiring of you with this long tale.'

'I like to hear it,' said nurse; and so did Betty, though a good deal of it was incomprehensible to her. She sat with Prince in her arms on the grass close by, and her quick little ears were listening to every word.

'Well,' said Mrs. Crump, with a sigh, 'there ain't much more to tell. Jane says Mrs. Fairfax shuts herself up and won't see a single visitor; Miss Grace, the eldest daughter, who was never very strong, has become a confirmed invalid, with very crotchety and fidgety ways, and makes every one miserable who comes near her. Miss Nesta is the only one that keeps bright; and Jane says her temper is that sweet, she bears with all her sister's crossness and unreasonableness, and her mother's icy coldness, like an angel. She have had her troubles, too, poor thing! Jane tells me that it was Mrs. Fairfax made her break off her engagement with her lover; he were some relative of the gentleman that lost the cheque, and she wouldn't have the engagement go on on no account. Jane says her lover had a talk with Mrs. Fairfax, and he were rather a high and mighty gentleman, and he left the room as white as death, and declared he would never set foot in the house again. Jane thinks Mrs. Fairfax was beside herself at the time, and must have insulted him fearful. Anyhow, it all came to an end. It's a world of trouble, Mrs. Duff. But I feel very sorry for Miss Nesta. The other ladies hardly ever leave the house or grounds, and they would like to keep Miss Nesta in as well; but she comes across to me and has a chat, and she reads a chapter and has prayers with grandfather. She's a very good young lady, and no one would think, to look at her, what she have come through.'

'Has she come through tribulation?' asked Betty, looking up suddenly.

'Well, I never did! To think of that child a-taking it all in!' ejaculated Mrs. Crump. 'What do you know about tribulation, little missy?'

'It means trouble or distress, I know;' and Betty's face was very wistful as she spoke.

'Run along and play with the others,' said nurse quickly, 'and don't worry your head over other people's troubles. There is plenty of it in the world, but your time hasn't come for it yet.'

'I wish it would come,' said Betty softly, 'and then I could put myself in that text.'

But only Prince heard the whispered words, and he wagged his tail in sympathy.

It was that night that Betty added another clause to her evening prayers. She generally said them aloud at nurse's knee, but it was not the first time that she had said, 'I want to whisper quite a secret to God'; and nurse always let her have her way.

'She is a queer little thing,' she told her brother; 'sometimes naughtier and more contrary than all the rest put together, and sometimes so angel-like that I wonder if she won't have an early death. But there's no knowing how to take her!'

Betty's secret was this,—

'And please, God, forgive Prince his sins and take him to heaven when he dies, and let me come through great tribulation, so that I may be like your people in heaven.'

When haymaking commenced at Brook Farm the children's delight knew no bounds. Every moment of the day they were out in the fields; and as the great cart-loads of hay were driven off, they felt proud and pleased with having helped in the work. Prince enjoyed it as much as any one; but he never left his little mistress's side for long. One evening, as the tired haymakers were resting, after having placed the last load on the wagon, Betty, dancing by the cart, was inspired to ascend the ladder which had been left against it.

'Come on,' she shouted to Douglas and Molly, 'and we'll have a ride home.'

Up they went, unnoticed by any, and danced up and down with delight when they reached the top. Then nurse discovered them, and in her fright and anxiety at their risky position she rushed towards them and screamed aloud. The horses, startled, swerved hastily aside, and Douglas, dangerously near the edge, over-balanced himself, and fell with a terrible thud to the ground. It was the work of a moment to seize him and drag him from the wheels, which mercifully did not touch him; but he was carried into the house stunned and insensible, and Molly and Betty, with scared, white faces, were taken down and sent indoors.

'It's your fault,' whispered Molly to the frightened Betty; 'you made us come up, and now Douglas will die! I think he's dead already; you'll be a murderer, and you'll be sent to prison and hung!'

And Betty quite believed this assertion, and crept up to the passage outside Douglas's bedroom trembling with excitement and fright. She crouched down in a corner, and Prince came up, put his two paws on her shoulder, and licked her face with a little wistful whine. It was a long time before nurse came out of the room, and then she wasted very few words on the little culprit.

'Go to bed, you naughty child, and tell Miss Molly to go too. You are never safe from mischief, and it's a mercy your brother hasn't been killed.'

'Will he get better, nurse?'

But nurse made no reply, and both little girls were long before they got to sleep that night, so fearful were their conjectures as to the fate of their brother.

Douglas was only stunned for the time, and very much bruised and shaken. Nurse kept him in bed for two or three days, and the two little girls were unremitting in their care and attention. He accepted their services with much complacency, and enjoyed his important and interesting position.

'What would you two girls have done if I had died?' he asked. 'Who would have been your leader then?'

'You're not my leader,' said Betty promptly. 'No one is my leader. I lead myself.'

'I don't know what I should have done,' said Molly pensively. 'I should have had to go about with Betty then. You see, I should have her, and the twins have themselves. I don't think Bobby and Billy would miss any of us much if we were to die. We should be equal if you died, Douglas—two and two, but I'm glad you're going to get better.'

'You wouldn't have gone about with me, Molly,' said Betty, with a decisive shake of her head, as she stooped to caress Prince at her feet, 'because you would have been one too many. We are two and two without you. I don't want any one with me but Prince. You would have to be the odd one if Douglas died—like I used to be.'

'Prince is only a dog,' said Molly, with a little curl of her lip. 'I wouldn't make two with a dog!'

Betty's eyes sparkled dangerously.

'Prince is ever so much nicer than you are—much nicer, and you're jealous because he likes me and not you. He's my very own, and I love him, and he loves me; and I love him better than all the people in the world put together, so there!'

'You needn't get in a temper. He's a silly, stupid kind of a dog, and Mr. Giles said yesterday if he caught him chasing his sheep round the field, he would give him a good beating; and I hope he will, for he nearly chased the sheep yesterday.'

'When you two have done fighting I should like to speak. My head aches. I think I should like some of the jelly nurse made for me. It will make it better.'

The little girls' rising wrath subsided. Both rushed to fulfil Douglas's desire,—for had not nurse left them in charge, and had she not also warned them against exciting him by loud talking and noise?

'I'm glad you will get better,' said Betty presently. 'I saw Miss Fairfax in church yesterday, and she asked me how you were.'

'What were you doing in church?' demanded Douglas. 'It wasn't Sunday.'

'Prince and I go to church very often,' said Betty, putting on a prim little air. 'We have several businesses there; but we don't tell every one what we do.'

'Do you play the organ?' asked Douglas, a little eagerly.

'No, but we hear it played, and we sing, and we—well, we do lots of other things.'

'I shall come with you next time you go,' and Douglas's tone was firm.

'No,' said Betty; 'you'll be one too many. I don't want Molly, and I don't want you. I've got Prince, and I don't want no one else.'

It was thus she aired her triumphs daily; and it was by such speeches that she revealed how much she had felt and suffered in times past by being so constantly left out in the cold. And Prince was daily becoming more and more companionable. Not one doubt did Betty ever entertain as to his not understanding or caring for her long confidences. He slept in a little basket at the foot of her bed. She was wakened by his wet kisses in the morning, and he liked nothing better than snuggling into bed with her. Tucking his little black nose under her soft chin, he would place a paw on each of her shoulders, and settle off into a reposeful sleep; whilst Betty would lie perfectly still, gazing at him with loving eyes, and every now and then giving him a gentle squeeze and murmuring, 'You're my very own, my darling, and I love you.'

CHAPTER VIII

GOD'S PATCHWORK

'Good-morning to you, little maid.'

Betty and Prince had been straying through the lanes, and had suddenly come upon the old sexton, who was leaning over his cottage gate smoking a short clay pipe.

Betty's face dimpled with smiles.

'May I come in and see your little house?' she asked. 'Prince and I want something to do. Douglas and Molly are lying in a hammock, and making up stories; and the twins are no company.'

'Come in, come in, my dear, and welcome, but 'tis a lonesome kind o' home with only me in it; 'twas very different once on a time.'

He led the way up a narrow path through rows of cabbages and sweet peas, and ushered her into a tiny kitchen, clean, but rather untidy. Betty looked round with a child's admiring eyes. There were great shells on the mantelpiece, a stuffed owl on a sideboard, and lots of other quaint curiosities on some shelves in a recess.

Then she climbed into a big rocking-chair.

'This is lovely,' she said; 'it's almost as good as a rocking-horse, if you go very fast.'

The old man stood looking at her for a minute; then seated himself on the low window-seat, and went on smoking. When Betty had swung herself violently to and fro for some minutes, she asked,—

'Have you been busy digging graves to-day?'

'No; 'tis a fortnight since I had one: the season has bin rare and healthy.'

'Then what have you been doing?' demanded the child.

'Oh, I don't let the time slip by; there are a many things I turn my hand to. I digs my taters up, and gardens a bit first thing in the morning, and I cleans up in my churchyard, and then I cooks a bit o' dinner, and has a bit o' gossip with my neighbours. I'm a sociable sort o' chap, though I'm so lonesome. And I has a bit o' reading on occasions. Are you a-thinkin' any more o' that 'ere tex' that we was a-argufying on t'other arter-noon?'

Betty nodded.

'I'm always thinking of it,' she said, stopping the motion of the chair, and looking up at him with grave, earnest eyes.

'Ah, well, so am I! I've had a good bit o' readin', too, 'tis a most important thing, the Bible be; and I've been giving a good bit o' my mind to it latterly. 'Twas your calm tone of saying I must be ready to die, if I'd bin through tribbylation, started me off. I couldn't quite make out about the washing, and so I've a looked it up. And I've found out from the old Book that I'm as black a sinner as ever lived on this 'ere blessed earth.'

'How dreadful!' Betty said in an awed, shocked tone; 'and you told me you were so good! I never knew grown-up people were wicked; I thought it was only children. What made you find it out?'

'Well, 'twas readin' what we ought to live like, first knocked me down. I got a-lookin' through them there epistlies, and got awful cast down. And then I thinks to mysel', p'raps arter all Paul and such like were too severe, so I went to the gospels, for I've always heerd the gospels tell of love, and not judgment, but I wasn't comforted by them, not a bit,—not even when I turned up the sheep chapter that I used for to learn as a little 'un. It says there, "My sheep hear My voice, and I know them, and they follow Me." And I says to myself, "Reuben! you've never a listened to His voice; you've a gone your own way all your life through, and you ain't a follered Him one day in all the sixty-and-eight years you've a bin on this 'ere blessed earth!" Well, I began to think I'd better say that prayer my dear old missis a told me, "Wash me, and I shall be whiter than snow." And then 'twas last Toosday night about seven o'clock I got the answer.'

The old man paused, took his pipe out of his mouth, and looked up at the blackened rafters across his little kitchen with a quivering smile about his lips; whilst Betty, with knitted brows, tried hard to follow him in what he was saying.

'I was a-turnin' over the leaves of the old Book,' he continued, 'when I come to a tex' which stared me full in the face, and round it was pencilled a thick black line, which was the doin' of my missis. I'll read it for you, little maid.'

84   Amy Le Feuvre

He rose, and took from the shelf a large family Bible. Placing it on the table, he turned over its leaves with a trembling hand; and then his voice rang out with a solemn triumph in it, '"Come, now, and let us reason together, saith the Lord: though your sins be as scarlet, they shall be as white as snow; though they be red like crimson, they shall be as wool." My knees began to tremble, for I says to myself, "Reuben, 'tis the Lord's voice to thee." And I drops down on the floor, just where you're a-sittin', missy, and I says, "Amen, so be it, Lord." I gets up with a washed soul—washed in the blood of the Lamb.'

There was silence; the old man's attitude, his upward gaze, his solemn emphasis, awed and puzzled Betty.

'And now you're in the text!' she said at last, somewhat wistfully; as she drew Prince to her, and lifted him into her lap.

'I shall be one o' these days, for certain sure,' was old Reuben's reply; 'but 'tis the Lord that will put me there; 'tis His washing that has done it.'

'That's what Miss Fairfax said; she said it wasn't tribulation would bring us to heaven. She made me sing,—

"There was no other good enough
To pay the price of sin;
He only could unlock the gate
Of heaven and let us in."

But I'm quite sure God won't mean me to stand in the middle of those people round the throne, if I haven't been through tribulation; I'm quite sure He won't! I shall find myself in a mistake if I try to creep in among them; and, oh! I want to be there, I want to be there!'

Tears were welling up, and Prince wondered why he was clutched hold of so convulsively by his little mistress. Reuben looked at her, rubbed his head a little doubtfully, and then straightened himself up with a sudden resolve.

'Look here, little maid; you just a foller me: I'm a-goin' to the church.'

Up Betty sprang, her tears were brushed away; and she and Prince danced along by the side of the old man, her doubts and fears dispersing for the time.

But Reuben was very silent. He led her into the cool, dark church and up the side aisle to the tomb of little Violet Russell. There he stopped, and directed the child's gaze above it to the stained-glass window.

'Can you read the tex', little maid?'

'Yes,' said Betty brightly; 'why, even Bobby and Billy know that: "Suffer the little children to come unto Me, and forbid them not."'

'And that's what the Lord says,' the old man went on; 'did He say the children were to have tribbylation afore they comed to Him? Why, for sure not! And if you, little missy, go straight into His arms when you gets to heaven, you'll be safe enough, and He'll know where to put you.'

Betty's little face beamed all over.

'And He will love me, even if I haven't been through tribulation?'

'Why, for sure He will.'

Amy Le Feuvre

Betty gave a happy little sigh.

'I tell you what, now,' Reuben added; 'if you're a-wantin' to have tribbylation made clear to you, I'll take you down to see old Jenny—praychin' Jenny, she used to be called—for she used to hold forth in chapel bettern than a parson. And she's bin bedridden these twelve year; but she can learn anybody about the Bible; she knows tex's by thousands; there hain't no one can puzzle Jenny over the Bible.'

'Is she very ill?' asked Betty.

'She's just bedridden with rheumatics, that's all; but 'tis quite enough; and I was calkilatin' only t'other day that I'll have to be diggin' her grave afore Christmas.'

'Will you take me to see her now?'

'For sure I will.'

Out of the cool church they went, and along the hot, dusty road, till they reached a low thatched cottage by the wayside. Reuben lifted the latch of the door, and walked right in.

There was a big screen just inside the door, and a voice asked at once,—

'Who be there?'

"Tis only Reuben and a little lass that wants to see you.' And Betty was led round the screen to a big four-post bed with spotlessly clean hangings and a wonderful patch-work quilt. Lying back on the pillows was one of the sweetest old women that Betty had ever seen. A close frilled night-cap surrounded a cheery, withered face—a face that looked as if nothing would break the placid smile upon it, nothing would dim the joy and peace shining through the faded blue eyes.

Betty held out her little hand.

'How do you do?' she said; 'this old man has brought me to see you. He said you would tell me about tribulation.'

'Bless your dear little heart! Lift her up on the foot of the bed, Reuben. Why, what a bonny little maid! and who may she be?'

'She be lodgin' at Farmer Giles's; and be troubled in her mind concarning tribbylation.'

The old woman reached over, and laid a wrinkled hand on the soft, childish one.

'Then tell old Jenny, dearie, what it is.'

Betty was quite ready to do so; and poured forth such a long, incoherent story that it was very difficult to understand her. Jenny did not quite take in her perplexity.

'Ay, dearie, most of us has tribbylation in some form or t'other; I often think, as I lie lookin' at my patchwork quilt, that it be just a pictur' of our life—a little bit o' brightness and then a patch of dark; but the dark is jined to the bright, and one never knows just what the next patch will be. But the One who makes it knows—He's a-workin' in the pattern, and the black dark bits only serve to show up the bright that's a-comin'.'

'Ay,' said Reuben, sinking into a chair; 'I mind plenty o' black days in my life; but I've had a many bright 'uns too— ay, and one white 'un, and that were last Toosday! It be a fine patch o' white in my quilt, Jenny!'

'Tribbylation!' said the old woman musingly; 'I mind o' several verses on it: "In the world ye shall have tribbylation; but be of good cheer: I have overcome the world." "We must through much tribbylation enter into the Kingdom of God." "We glory in tribbylation also, knowing that tribbylation worketh patience." "Who shall separate us from the love of Christ? shall tribbylation?" Ah, tribbylation is tryin' to the flesh, but 'tis for the improvin' of the soul!'

'And does everybody have it except children?' asked Betty with a solemn face.

'I think as how most folks have it in one form or t'other; the saints get it surely, for "whom the Lord loveth He chasteneth, and scourgeth every son whom He receiveth."'

'What does "chasteneth" mean?'

'Punish, I take it, dearie, your father and mother punishes you at times, don't they?'

'No, never; only nurse.'

'Ah, well; and doesn't she desire your good? She don't do it just to spite you.'

'I s'pose it's for my good,' said Betty doubtfully.

'Tribbylation will allays be a mystery,' went on the old woman, speaking more to Reuben than the child. 'We must bow our heads and take it, whether we like it or no; and it's wonderful strange how differently folks take it! Seems to me, as the Bible puts it, it's just a fire, and whiles some like wax gets melted and soft by it, t'others are like the clay, they gets hard and unbendable. I've known lots o' both those sorts in my time; 'tis only by keeping close to the Hand that smites

Odd   89 that you feels the comfort and healing that goes along with it. If you keeps a distance off, and lets the devil come a-sympathisin' and a-groanin' with you, then it's all bitterness through and through.'

'Ay,' said Reuben, 'me and the devil have oft sat down together over my troubles; and he do know how to make 'em werry black!'

Betty's round eyes and puzzled gaze at this assertion made Reuben adopt another tone.

'But here's this little lass, Jenny, a-wantin' to have tribbylation, for fear she shouldn't be one o' the Lord's people after all.'

The old woman looked across at the child, and then she nodded brightly at her.

'And you shall have it, dearie; the Lord will send it surely; and when you're in the midst o't, you mind these words o' the Lord's, "Be thou faithful unto death, and I will give thee a crown of life." It's in tribbylation our faith fails; we can't see in the dark, and we mistrust our Guide.'

Betty's face lit up at these words, and she brushed away some glittering drops from her long lashes.

'You think I shall really have it?' she questioned eagerly.

'Surely you will in some form or t'other, and p'raps before you're a growed-up woman. I sometimes think little folks' troubles are as big as the older folks.'

Betty did not hear much more of the conversation that followed. Old Jenny had done more to comfort and satisfy her than any one else, and she left the cottage with Reuben, saying,—

'I like Jenny very much, and so does Prince; we will come and see her again.'

CHAPTER IX

BETTY'S DISCOVERY

Molly and Douglas were up in an apple tree in the orchard late one afternoon, when Betty and Prince came rushing by.

'Hullo, where are you going?' shouted Douglas.

Betty came to a standstill, and Prince likewise, the latter putting his tongue out and looking up inquiringly, as he panted for breath.

Betty cut a caper. 'I'm going to spend the day with Miss Fairfax to-morrow; me and Prince, hurray!'

And Prince danced round his little mistress's legs with delighted barks.

'I don't believe it,' said Molly, looking down through the leafy branches; 'didn't she ask us too?'

'No, only me; she said she'd ask you another day.'

'Where did you see Miss Fairfax?'

'In church; she has been making the loveliest music, and

Prince and I have been singing.'

'Prince singing!' said Douglas contemptuously; 'I should like to hear him!'

'He does,' Betty said eagerly; 'he really does. He kind of whines in his throat and up his nose, and sometimes he puts up his head, opens his mouth wide, and gives a lovely howl! And he looks awfully pleased when he's done it; he thinks he sings very nicely. Where's nurse?'

'She's washing Bobby; he tumbled right into the pig-stye, and came out a disgusting objec'!'

'Is she rather cross?'

'Of course she is; she won't let you go to Miss Fairfax if you ask her now.'

'Then I'll wait till tea.'

Betty threw herself down on the grass, and Prince sat at her feet, thumping his tail on the ground, and watching intently every change that flitted across her face. Now and then he would make a snap at some flies; if Betty spoke to him, his whole body would wriggle with ecstasy; he seemed to live on her smiles and caressing words.

'It will be very dull to spend the day with a grown-up person,' said Douglas presently; 'I'm glad she didn't ask me; I never do care for grown-up persons.'

His lordly air in making this assertion helped to fortify Molly, who was bitterly disappointed in not being included in the invitation.

'I love her!' exclaimed Betty; 'she's the nicest grown-up I've ever seen. She does laugh so, and isn't a bit proper.'

'Well, you'll be sick of it before the day is over, you see if you aren't! Now Molly and I are going to have a lovely day. Would you like to know what we're going to do?'

Molly listened eagerly, for Douglas's plans were always sudden and unexpected.

'We're going off directly after breakfast with our dinner in our basket, and we're going down to the brook. I'm going to build a bridge over it at the widest part!'

Both sisters looked aghast at this audacity.

'What will you build it of?' questioned Betty sceptically.

'Of stones and clay. We shall make the clay down there; and I shall put a few boards in, and make it all smooth with some putty that I saw in the stable.'

'You will fall in the water and get drowned,' said Betty; and then she jumped up and ran off to the house, to escape a pelting shower of small green apples from her irate brother.

Nurse made a few objections at first, when she heard of Betty's invitation; but when she knew that Miss Fairfax was going to call for her little guest, and had promised to bring her safely back again, she gave the required permission; and Betty's sleep that night was full of wonderful dreams about her coming visit.

She woke very early the next morning, and was full of confidences to Prince of all that they were going to do and say. She gave nurse no rest after breakfast until she had dressed her in her best white frock and tan shoes and stockings; then, with her large white Leghorn hat and little white silk gloves, she sat up on a chair in the best front parlour, feeling very important, and making a dainty little picture as she sat there. Prince had a piece of pink ribbon tied round his neck; Mrs. Giles had produced it from her work-basket, and had gained a fervent kiss and hug from the little maiden thereby.

At last Nesta arrived in a low pony carriage, to Betty's intense delight. She wished that Molly and Douglas had waited to see her step in and drive off, but they had run off half an hour before, nurse having packed them a lunch-basket, as desired.

Nesta smiled at the excited child, as she and Prince tumbled themselves into the carriage with a good deal of fuss; but when they were once off, driving through the shady lanes, Betty folded her little hands demurely round Prince in her lap, and upon her face came that dreamy look her friend so loved to see. She did not ask questions, and the drive was a quiet one, until they at length drove through some iron gates round a thick shrubbery, and up to a big white house with green Venetian shutters, and a brilliant show of roses in front. Betty was lifted out, and taken up some low stone steps into a broad old-fashioned hall. It seemed very cool and quiet inside; thick soft rugs lay about the tiled floor, large pots of flowering shrubs stood here and there, and at the farther end was an open door with striped awning outside, and a glimpse of a smooth grassy lawn and bright flower-beds.

Nesta opened a door, and led Betty into a darkened room, full of sweet scents of heliotrope and roses.

'Now I am going to bring you something, so sit down and

wait for me.'

Betty's quick eyes were taking in everything; and as for Prince, his nose was as busy as his eyes, and a low growl and a stiffening of his ears soon told his little mistress that he had discovered something objectionable. When Betty crossed the room on tip-toe, she found him in front of a large mirror, and the snarl on his lips was not pleasant to see, as he faced his mock antagonist.

'Oh, Prince, for shame! I must hold you; what would I do if you broke that glass? Now come and look at these beautiful pictures. Look at that lady up there; she has got a little dog in her arms very like you.'

It was a pleasant morning-room, with plenty of pretty ornaments scattered about, and after the farm kitchen it had a great fascination for Betty.

Nesta presently returned with some sponge cakes and a glass of raspberry vinegar, which Betty found most refreshing.

'Do you live here all alone?' she asked.

'No,' said Miss Fairfax, smiling; 'I have my mother and sister here. My mother is not very well to-day, but I will take you to see my sister now. Come along, this way; will Prince be good?'

'Yes, he won't bark at all unless he meets another dog.'

Betty trotted along, following her guide across the hall to another room, where on a couch near the window lay a lady.

'I've brought a little visitor to see you, Grace,' Nesta said in cheery tones. 'This is the little girl I was telling you about the other day.'

'I can't bear children,' was the fretful reply; 'why do you bring her here?'

But nevertheless she put the book down that she was reading, and scanned the child from head to foot. Betty's grave face and earnest scrutiny in return seemed to vex her more.

'How children stare! Do you think me a scarecrow, child? can't you keep your eyes to yourself? What is your name?'

'Betty,' and the little girl drew to her friend's side rather shyly.

'Go and shake hands,' whispered Nesta.

Betty went up to the couch and held out her little hand. The invalid took it, and the fair, flushed little face seemed to attract her.

'This is a perfect baby, Nesta; I thought you meant a much older child. Well, little girl, haven't you a tongue in your head? Have you nothing to say? It's the way of this house: here I lie from morning to night without a soul to speak to, and if I do have a visitor it is half a dozen words, and then off they go! I should like them to lie here and suffer as I do—perhaps they might have a little more feeling for an invalid if they did.'

'Are you going to die?' asked Betty timidly.

'Take her away!' gasped Miss Grace; 'don't bring a child to mock me; and I suppose you will be devoting yourself to her the whole day, and I shall have no one to read the paper to me.'

'No,' said Nesta brightly, 'I am going to let her play in the garden, and then I shall come to you as usual. Come along, Betty; now you and Prince can have a scamper.'

Out into the garden they went; but Betty rubbed her eyes in bewilderment when she got there. Surely she had seen this garden before! Was it in her dreams last night?

She tripped across the velvet lawn, answering Nesta's questions and remarks rather absently, and then suddenly she turned round with a beaming face. 'I've been here before,' she said; 'I had some lilies from over there, and I came through that little door in the wall from the wood. Do you know my lady? She looks like a queen. Does she live with you?'

Nesta looked perfectly bewildered.

'You must be dreaming, Betty. How could you have come here? When did you come?'

Betty told her of her adventure in the wood, and Nesta listened in wonder.

'It must have been my mother, and yet I can hardly understand it. It is unlike her to take any notice of children.' Then she added, 'Do you think you can make yourself happy in the garden, Betty, or would you like to go down the green walk outside the little gate?'

'Will you open the gate and let me see?' said Betty thoughtfully.

Nesta took her to it, and then for a moment they stood silent, looking down the green avenue, with the golden sunshine glinting through the leafy trees, and the tall bracken swaying to and fro in the summer breeze.

Amy Le Feuvre

'Which do you like best, Betty—the garden or this?'

Betty turned and looked behind her at the lovely flowers and beautifully kept grass and gravel walks, and then she heaved a little sigh as she looked out into the wood.

'My beautiful old lady asked me that question before, and I thought then I liked the garden, but now I like this green walk best,' she said.

'You prefer nature uncultivated, don't you? So do I. But I do not often come out here. This is my mother's favourite spot.'

'Did you say "Nature"?' questioned betty eagerly. 'Do you mean Mother Nature? You said you would show her to me one day.'

'So I did, I have quite forgotten. Well, there she is out there, Betty. Nature is God's beautiful earth: the country, the birds, the rabbits, and the squirrels—everything that He makes and that man leaves alone.'

'I don't understand;' and the child's white brow was creased with puckers. 'I thought she was a woman: Mr. Roper said she was; he said he had learnt many a lesson from her.'

'And so have I,' said Nesta softly. 'Listen, Betty. Sometimes I have gone out of doors tired and worried and sad; I have wandered through the wood, and the sweet sounds and sights I have seen in it have brought me home rested and refreshed. They have spoken to me of God's love, and God's care, and God's perfection. You are too little to understand me, I expect, but you will when you get older. God makes everything beautiful, and He watches over the tiny birds and insects whom no one but Himself ever sees. The tiniest flower is noticed by Him, and all His works in nature lead us to think of Him, and to remember how He loves and cares for us.'

Betty's blue eyes were raised earnestly upwards.

'God does love everything, doesn't He? And He loves Prince just as much as He does you and me.'

Nesta hesitated. 'I think, darling, God has a different love for us to what He has for animals. We have cost the dear Saviour His life; our souls have been redeemed. Animals have no souls, they do not know the difference between right and wrong—'

'But Prince does,' broke in Betty hastily; 'he knows lots of the Bible, for I've told him about it, and I read The Peep of Day to him on Sunday. He likes it; he lies quite still on my lap and folds his paws and listens like anything. And I've told him about Jesus dying for him, and how he must try to be good. And he does try: he wanted to run after some little chickens yesterday, and I called him and told him it was wicked, and he came away from them directly; and I know he wanted to go after them dreadfully, for he was licking his lips and glaring at them!'

This outburst from Betty was too much for Nesta. She looked at her with perplexity, then wisely turned the subject, and after a few minutes' more chat left her, and went back to the house.

Betty wandered out into the wood, and then seating herself on a soft bank surrounded by ferns and foxgloves, she drew Prince to her.

'Come, you little darling, how do you like this? Isn't it lovely to be spending a day in that lovely house, and not have to be shut out with only some lilies to take away? Do you like it, Prince? And do you think we shall see that nice queen, and find out if she sent you in a basket to me? Do you understand about nature, Prince? I wish I did, but it's the earth, I think; you put your mouth down and kiss it. Isn't it nice and soft?'

And then, laying her curly head on the velvet moss, Betty pressed her lips to it, whispering, 'Mother Nature, Mr. Roper sent you his love and a kiss!'

Prince was not content to stay as quiet as this for long, and when a rabbit popped out from a hole close by, he was after it like lightning. Betty tore after him delightedly, and a scamper removed from her busy little mind for the time thoughts that were beginning to trouble her.

When Nesta returned to the garden half an hour after, she found Betty deep in conversation with the old gardener, and Prince was hunting for snails in a thick laurel hedge close by.

'We didn't stay out in the wood very long,' Betty explained; 'we got tired of running after rabbits.'

'You must come in to luncheon now; I want you to come up to my room to wash your face and hands.'

'Will the cross lady be at lunch?' asked Betty, as she trotted up the broad oak stairs a few minutes later.

'Hush, dear; she is ill, remember. I don't think she will lunch with us.'

Nesta took her little visitor through a long passage to a pretty bedroom, and Betty looked about at all the pictures and knick-knacks, asking ceaseless questions, and fingering everything that she could get hold of. Her curls were brushed out, her hands and face washed, and then she was brought down to the large drawing-room.

'This is my little friend, mother,' said Nesta, going in.

A tall figure turned round from the window, and Betty saw her mysterious lady once again. She looked colder and sterner than ever, and put up her gold pince-nez to scan the little new-comer down; but Betty's radiant face, dimpling all over with pleasure as she held up her face for a kiss, brought a softer gleam to the old grey eyes, and, to her daughter's astonishment, Mrs. Fairfax stooped to give the expected kiss.

'It is the little trespasser,' she said. 'I did not know I should see you again so soon.'

Then she turned to Nesta. 'Grace informed me she intended to lunch with us. She is in the dining-room already, so we will wait no longer.'

They walked in silence across to the dining-room, and Betty, awed by the big table, the noiseless butler, and the cold, formal stateliness of the meal, sat up in her big chair, subdued and still.

CHAPTER X

A LITTLE MESSENGER

Miss Fairfax seemed the most talkative, but her conversation was a perpetual flow of complaints; the food, the weather, and her ailments were her chief topics, and Betty's round eyes of amazement, as she sat opposite, served to irritate her more. At length she gave a little start and scream.

'I am sure there is a dog in the room!' she exclaimed. 'How often I have told you, Jennings' (this to the butler), 'to keep the dogs out of our rooms!'

'It's my dog,' said Betty at once; 'it's only Prince; he always sits under my chair; he's such a dear, he waits as quiet as a mouse.'

'Take him out of the room at once, Jennings; I can't eat another mouthful while he is here. You ought never to have allowed him to come in!'

'Oh, Grace, he won't hurt you!' said Nesta, remonstrating.

Miss Fairfax put her knife and fork together, and leant back in her chair.

'Very well; as my nerves are never considered in the least, it is useless for me to speak; I had better go back to my room. I am continually being urged to join you at meal-times; yet, when I do, I am expected to go through the misery of having a wretched dog crawling round my feet, and setting every nerve in my head quivering and throbbing.'

'Take the dog outside,' said Mrs. Fairfax quietly; then, turning to Betty, who looked very perturbed and flushed, she said, 'Jennings will take care of him, and he shall have some dinner in the kitchen.'

'He won't be beaten, will he? He didn't know it was wrong to follow me'; and Betty's eyes began to fill with tears, as she saw Prince seized by the scruff of his neck, and carried off, in spite of indignant growls and snaps.

'No, he won't be beaten,' she was assured; but after this she had no appetite for her dinner; and when the ladies rose from the table she ran up to Mrs. Fairfax.

'May I have Prince again now? He's so very good. I want him dreadfully.'

'Yes, he shall be brought to you. What are you going to do with the child, Nesta?'

'I will take her out into the garden, mother. But I hear old Mrs. Parr has come up for some linseed meal I promised her. Her husband is very ill again with bronchitis. I shall not be gone long.'

'Then Betty shall come upstairs with me.'

Again Nesta wondered, but wisely said nothing.

Amy Le Feuvre

Prince came scampering across the hall, and Betty, now completely happy, took hold of Mrs. Fairfax's hand, and went upstairs into a lovely little boudoir, where she sat down in a low cushioned seat by the window, and chattered away to her heart's content.

'Did you send Prince to me? You did, didn't you? I knew it was you! He is such a darling, and it makes me into a couple—which I've never been before.'

Mrs. Fairfax smiled; she seemed to lose some of her stiffness when with Betty alone.

'And is he as much a companion as another brother or sister might be?'

'I think he's much nicer. I wouldn't have any one instead of him for all the world.'

'What have you been doing with yourself since I saw you?'

'Lots and lots of things. I go to church to hear Miss Fairfax play the organ; and I take flowers to dead Violet; and I have got into lots of scrapes; but I don't think I'm quite as naughty here as I used to be in London. At least, we can't quite make it out. Douglas was saying the other day, nurse lets him climb any trees here; but if he tried to climb a lamp-post, or even one of the trees in the parks, in London, he was always being whipped or put into cells for it! And in the country we can go out without gloves, and run races along the roads, and swing on gates, and we never get punished at all. We don't want to go back to London; it's so dreadfully hard to be good there.'

'But don't you want to see your father and mother again?'

'Yes, I s'pose so; but we don't see them very much in London. I'd like to stay in the country for ever and ever, and so would Prince.' After a pause she went on, 'You see, there's a good deal more going on in the country than in London. We know a lot more people, and there's always something fresh happening. Now, in London every day is the same, and we have only the nursery to play in, we get so tired of it. At the farm where we live we're always having nice surprises; lots of little calves are born quite suddenly, or little horses, and we don't know anything about it till we go and see them in the morning. Yesterday there were six little black pigs, such little beauties! And then we have so many more people to talk to. There's Farmer and Mrs. Giles, and Sam, and all the carters, and the old man who digs the graves, and old Jenny, and you, and Miss Fairfax, and Mr. Russell, but I've only seen him once.'

Betty paused for breath.

'And what do you find to talk about to so many people?'

'I've been talking rather grave talks with some of them,' Betty said reflectively, 'about tribulation.'

Mrs. Fairfax raised her eyebrows.

'That is very grave talk indeed for such a mite as you. What do you know about it?'

'I know that everybody has got it except me, and I want to have it; and old Jenny said I'd be sure to come to it soon. She's had it, and Reuben has, and Mr. Russell, and nurse, and Miss Fairfax has. Has the cross lady downstairs had it, and have you?'

Mrs. Fairfax's lips quivered a little as she turned away her

Amy Le Feuvre

head. The soft, childish fingers were probing the wound, and she shrank from their touch.

Betty went on dreamily, 'I often wonder what it's like, and whether you feel like Christian did in the dark valley; but he got through it all right at last! I should like to come right through it into the middle of the text, and Jenny says I shall some day!'

There was glad triumph in her tone.

'What text?' asked Mrs. Fairfax, looking out of the window, and away to the green woods in the distance.

Betty repeated once more the familiar words,—

'"These are they which came out of great tribulation, and have washed their robes, and made them white in the blood of the Lamb." How glad they must be to have had it! don't you think so?'

And then the stately Mrs. Fairfax sat down, and took Betty upon her knee; drawing her close to her, till she had the little dark curly head resting against her shoulder, she bent her head to hers, and said, almost passionately,—

'God grant you will never know such trouble as mine, little one—trouble that turns your heart to stone, and blots all heaven from your sight!'

Betty put her little arms round her neck.

'Old Jenny said I should have it,' she repeated, 'and she told me when I was in the middle of it to remember, "Be thou faithful unto death"—I forget the other part.'

There was silence for some moments; then Mrs. Fairfax kissed the upturned face.

'Now run downstairs, little woman, and find Nesta. I will say good-bye now, for I shall not see you again.'

Betty obeyed instantly, and when she had gone, for the first time for many a long month, the sorrowful woman knelt in prayer. 'God help me!' she cried; 'I have been an unfaithful servant, and have refused to turn to Thee for comfort.'

The rest of the afternoon was as delightful as the morning to Betty. She visited the stables and poultry yard; she picked strawberries, and ate them whilst she picked; she gathered a large nosegay of flowers to take home to nurse; and then, at four o'clock, she came in to a delicious little tea in the cool, shady drawing-room. Miss Fairfax was lying on the sofa there, but she seemed to like to hear the child talk, and even condescended to allow Prince to come inside to receive a lump of sugar on his nose, whilst he sat up and begged.

'I've had a lovely day,' said Betty, as Nesta was putting on her hat upstairs in the bedroom.

'And so have I,' responded Nesta, laughing. 'You have been very good company, Betty; I shall be quite dull when you are gone.'

'Have you no one to talk to, when I'm not here? Are you an odd one?'

'Perhaps I may be.'

Why don't you make yourself into a couple with some one, like Prince and me?'

But this made Nesta's soft eyes fill with tears; and Betty felt very uncomfortable until she was kissed and told she was the funniest little chatterbox living. The pony carriage came round; and a little later she was being driven home, rather tired, and very happy, at her day's outing.

Nesta left her at the gate, and drove silently home. Betty had brought a good deal of brightness into her life; and though she was always outwardly so cheery in her manner, her heart was often heavy and sore. It was not a cheerful house; and as an hour later she tried to enliven the solemn dinner-table, expecting as usual to meet with no response, but grumbles from Grace and chilling indifference on the part of her mother, she was surprised by Mrs. Fairfax's efforts to take part in the conversation.

'That child is an original character,' she observed. 'Do you know who they are, Nesta?'

'Yes, Mr. Crump was telling me the other day; their father is the Member for Stonycroft, and their mother that Mrs. Stuart who is so busy in philanthropical objects in town. She was one of the Miss Champneys, the clever Miss Champneys, as we used to call them. I think the children must inherit the talents of their parents, for though they are regular little pickles for mischief, they are all original in their way. Betty thinks the most, I should say, the others seem to live in dreamland half their time. I came across the other girl and boy in an old willow tree the other day. I spoke to them, but was hushed up at once by the boy, who put his fair curly head out of the branches, and said, "You're not to speak to us just now; we're hiding from the Queen of the Brook! she comes dashing down in foam, she's so angry with us; and if she splashes us we shall be turned into black dogs, and have to go on all fours till dinner time!" I laughed and left them. I don't altogether envy their nurse!'

'Betty is not enough of a child,' Mrs. Fairfax said; 'some of her sayings are quite uncanny.'

'Do you think so? She has plenty of life and spirits. But she is a child of intense feeling. I am afraid she will suffer for it as she grows older. Yesterday I came upon her outside the churchyard crying, as if her heart would break, over a dead frog. I tried to comfort her. "Oh," she sobbed; "I'm so afraid Prince has killed it. I didn't see him, but he may have; and he doesn't look a bit sorry. What shall I do if he grows up a murderer!"'

Mrs. Fairfax would have thought Betty a stranger child still, if she could have seen her that evening tossing in her little bed.

Molly was fast asleep; nurse had left the room, and all was quiet; but Betty was going over in her busy little mind the events of the past day. At last she stretched out her hand to Prince in his basket.

'She said you had no soul, Prince; I wonder if you haven't! I wish you'd say prayers to God; I'm sure God will give you a soul, if you ought to have one! Prince, wake up!'

Prince rolled over, shook himself, and jumped up on the bed, wondering what was the reason of this summons.

Betty sat up with flushed cheeks and bright eyes. 'Come here. Prince! Now beg! that's right. Now say a prayer; just a very little one. I pray for you, darling, every night; but you're big enough to pray yourself. God will know your language if you speak to Him, and you can just speak secret to Him—I do often. Now, Prince—no—don't lick my hand, and keep your tail still. I wish you'd shut your eyes. I'll put my hand over them—there! Now Prince, ask God to give you a soul, and forgive your sins, and take you to heaven when you die.'

Betty bent her head in silence; whilst for two minutes Prince kept perfectly still; then she took her little hands from his eyes, and he gave a quick short bark of delight, perhaps in anticipation of a lump of sugar for this new trick taught him. If so, he was disappointed, he was only kissed and put back into his basket. And Betty laid her little head on the pillow, but only half satisfied. 'O God,' she murmured sleepily, 'if Prince hasn't prayed properly, please forgive him, and give him a soul and make him a good dog, for Jesus Christ's sake. Amen.'

CHAPTER XI

A DARING FEAT

It was a hot afternoon in July. The children had tired themselves out with play, and were resting under some shady trees near the farm. By and bye Betty wandered off into a neighbouring cornfield, and resting her head against an old log of wood in the corner of it, went fast asleep, whilst Prince sat at her feet, keeping a faithful watch over his little mistress. Mr. Russell, sauntering through a footpath in the field, came up and looked at them; and his artist's eye was at once charmed with the picture they made. He stood, and taking out his sketch-book, drew a rapid outline of Betty's little figure as she lay there, one hand grasping some red poppies, and the other arm thrown behind her curly head. Prince was also sketched; and then Betty awoke. She looked confused at first, then jumped to her feet.

'Don't be frightened,' said Mr. Russell gravely. 'Do you live near here?'

Betty pointed out the farm.

'And do you think you would be allowed to come to my house one day, for me to make a picture of you?'

112   Amy Le Feuvre

Betty coloured with pleasure.

'I'll ask nurse. All by myself?'

'All by yourself—at least with your dog. Where is your nurse? Would she come out here to speak to me?'

Nurse was only in the next field, so was easily fetched, and though demurring somewhat at first, was soon reassured by Mr. Russell, who promised to keep her only about an hour.

'I will see she returns to you safely, my good woman; and when you find that she has come to no harm, perhaps you will allow her to come again. I want to make a little sketch of her, for a subject I have in view.'

And it was settled that Betty should go to him the next day at two o'clock.

'I don't quite like it,' said nurse afterwards, when talking it over with Mrs. Giles; 'but he seemed rather a high-handed gentleman, as if he wouldn't take no. I don't know whether the mistress would like it, most children would be shy of it, but none of these seem to know what shyness is; and Miss Betty seems to make friends wherever she goes. I can't understand it; Miss Molly, to my eyes, is much the most taking!'

'Mr. Russell is our landlord,' responded Mrs. Giles; 'he's a proper sort o' gentleman, and he won't hurt the child by a-paintin' of her. He lives all alone since his little girl died, and maybe she'll cheer him up; he's very downhearted, folks say.'

'Why should you go and not us?' said Molly, when Betty ran off to tell them all about it; 'it's too bad; you're getting all the nice things, and I'm the eldest.'

'I don't expect you'll like it,' said Douglas, rolling over on the grass and tickling Bobby's bare legs with a bunch of grass; 'I know the man, and he has an awful temper! Sam told me he thrashed a boy who was taking a bird's nest out of his orchard; and he has a large glass room with skeletons and bits of people's bodies lying all about. I think he likes to get children in there, and then he keeps them prisoners, and never lets them out again.'

Betty stood still, eyeing her brother doubtfully.

'I don't believe it.'

'You wait till he gets you there! He has dead men's legs and hands. Sam says he's seen them through the window! He's a Bluebeard; he always keeps the room locked, and doesn't let any one in. And if he takes you in there to-morrow afternoon, you'll never come out again!'

'And then I shall have Prince, and take him back to London for my dog,' put in Molly.

'Prince is coming with me,' Betty retorted; 'so if I never come back again, Prince won't! And I don't care if we don't come back. I'd rather live with Mr. Russell than with you when you are cross.'

'He'll fatten you up with porridge for a week; and then he'll cut you up into little bits, and Prince too.'

Betty laughed and danced away, Prince at her heels.

'You're jealous because I'm going to be put into a picture,' she called out. 'I'll tell you all about the dead men's legs when I come back.'

The next afternoon she was taken up to the Hall by nurse, who arrayed herself in her best clothes, and was delighted when she was taken to the housekeeper's room to be entertained. She would have liked to wait there the full hour, but Mr. Russell had promised to bring back Betty himself; so she had not that excuse.

And Douglas and Molly were consoling themselves at home, by building a hay castle in the meadow, and capturing Bobby and Billy at intervals, under the plea of painting their pictures; and then going through a process which was more entertaining to them than to their little victims—that of cutting off their arms and legs to hang on their walls.

It was nearly five o'clock when Betty returned, and her little tongue was busy all tea-time.

'Such a funny room! and Mr. Russell had changed his mind, and he isn't going to paint my picture; but he's going to make a dead figure of me and Prince instead; he's got some white wet stuff like putty, and he rolls up his shirt-sleeves like a workman! I had to lie down and pretend to be asleep, but I could keep my eyes open, and I did see some legs, but they're images—and there was a image without a head, a dead figure, you know. And there were beautiful curtains, and flowers, and rugs, and pictures half finished. It was rather an untidy room. I told Mr. Russell what you said, Douglas; and he laughed. He gave me some peaches, and then we had a nice grave talk coming home.'

This and more Betty revealed; and her visits to the Hall became very frequent as time wore on. If she enjoyed them, Mr. Russell did too, and yet she brought to him mingled feelings of pleasure and pain. He talked lightly to her, and put aside his stern moods whilst with her; but every now and then some childish gesture or tone would stab him with the memory of his little daughter, and his brows would contract and his voice falter at the remembrance.

One day he was called away from the studio, and for some time Betty was left alone.

When he returned, he found her lying flat on her chest, turning over the leaves of a book.

'What book have you got hold of?' he asked; 'something that seems to interest you.'

'It's Revelation,' said Betty, with a beaming face.

'The Bible? I did not remember I had one in the room; ah yes, I remember, it's here for its antique cover! Well, what do you make of Revelation?'

'Oh, I love it, don't you? I'm reading about the singing in heaven; and it says "ten thousand times ten thousand, and thousands of thousands." What crowds there will be! Mr. Russell, supposing heaven gets too small for all the people, what will happen?'

'I don't think there's a chance of that,' Mr. Russell said, smiling; 'it doesn't look as if many are bound there in the present age, at all events.'

'It says,' went on Betty, with her finger on the page, 'for Thou wast slain, and hast redeemed us to God by Thy blood, out of every kindred and tongue and people and nation; that takes in everybody, doesn't it, Mr. Russell?'

'Yes,' said Mr. Russell, looking down at the little figure on the floor, half humorously, half sadly; 'every one that wants to be taken in.'

'Why should any one want to be outside?' questioned the child.

Mr. Russell did not answer; he went to his outline and uncovered it. It was rapidly progressing. Betty's little figure was nearly finished. There was the gnarled log of wood against which she lay; and Prince's outline had already been commenced.

She jumped up and came over to look at it.

'It would make a beautiful grave, wouldn't it?' she said thoughtfully; 'I should like to have it put on the top of mine when I die.'

'Don't talk about dying, child!' was the hasty reply.

'I'm afraid I'm not ready,' said Betty, with a shake of her curly head; 'but I will be when I've been through tribulation! Mr. Russell, do you think a dog can go through tribulation?'

'No, I do not,' said Mr. Russell, laughing. Betty's views on her favourite text were by this time well known to him; and he generally treated her childish difficulties with respect; but this unexpected question was too much for him, and Betty's little face clouded over at his laugh. She was very silent after that, and went home with rather a wistful little face.

But all serious thoughts were dissolved at the news that awaited her. Molly rushed out, her long hair flying in the wind: 'I've got a letter from Uncle Harry, and he is coming to see us next week!'

'And he's going to spend a week with us; he's going to fish, and I shall fish too!' shouted Douglas.

'And Uncle Harry will have cwicket with us!' cried the twins.

'Of course he wrote to me, as I'm the eldest,' said Molly proudly; 'if you'll be very good I'll read you his letter.' And producing a very crumpled envelope from her pocket, she read:—

'DEAR MADAM MOLLY,—

'I have had orders from your respected parents to come down for an inspection of you all; so expect me Tuesday, the 27th inst. Tell nurse all complaints will be attended to, and puni-shment duly administered. She must get me a room some-where for a week, as I have heard there is good fishing in your neighbourhood. My love to doughty Douglas and the three B's.

'Your affectionate uncle, 'HARRY.

'P.S.—Tell nurse I shall bring a rod with me.'

'Isn't he a funny dear?' went on Molly. 'He pretends he's coming to punish us! Won't we have fun when he comes!'

'He doesn't know there are six of us now,' observed Betty, with sparkling eyes; 'I wonder what he will say to Prince.'

The children could do little else but talk about their uncle's coming visit for the next week; and when at last Tuesday arrived, they were in a great state of excitement. Nurse could hardly curb their turbulent spirits. Captain Stuart was adored by his little nephews and nieces, and his visits were always a golden time. At last, after rescuing Douglas from a farm wagon that he was driving off during the carter's absence, Molly and Betty from an infuriated sow that they were trying to wash under the pump, and Bobby and Billy from a hay-cutter they were meditating using, nurse locked up all the five in the garret, hoping they would be safe there until their uncle arrived. Prince was left outside; and all Betty's beseeching petitions that he might share their punishment were unheeded by nurse. So Prince crouched down outside the door, patiently keeping watch, and now and then responding to his little mistress's voice through the keyhole by sundry whines and barks.

'Nurse won't dare to put us in cells after to-day,' said Douglas wrathfully; 'she is just doing it to pretend to Uncle Harry that we're always in disgrace; and I hate her!'

'And I was going down to the brook to get some forget-me-nots, to put in Uncle Harry's room,' said Molly plaintively.

'It's wather nice being punished all together,' said Bobby, who always dreaded being left alone.

Betty said nothing; her curly head was out of one of the windows, and she was deep in thought. At last she drew it in.

'S'posing the house was to take fire, and we were all to be locked in here?' she suggested.

Molly looked quite frightened at the thought; but Douglas rose to the occasion, and he said triumphantly,—

'Yes, nurse would be in a pretty state then! Farmer Giles would rush off for a fire-engine; we would throw up the windows, and then I'd get out on the roof and make a speech. I'd remind nurse of all the nasty things she has said and done to us since we were babies; how she has said over and over again there never were such children in the world, and that we nearly drove her mad; and then I'd say she'd be sorry now when she was going to see us burnt before her eyes; and she would be sobbing and crying, and so would Mrs. Giles and Sam and all the others!'

'But they might get ladders to take us down,' suggested Molly.

'There's only one ladder long enough. Sam would put that up, but the flames underneath the floor would come out and burn the ladder in two; and there's no fire-escape! They don't seem to have them in the country. I should go on speaking as long as I could, and then I should say we didn't wish to go down to our graves angry, so we would forgive her, only we hoped the next children she had she would be kinder to. And then I would say good-bye; and the roof would be cracking underneath me; and nurse would scream and cry; and then I would take a leap right into the middle of the fire; and there would be a kind of explosion, and the house would fall in; and the next day there would be five heaps of bones and black ashes! all that was left of us! and nurse would sit down with a broken heart in the middle of us!'

Bobby and Billy had been listening to this awful story with their eyes nearly starting out of their heads; and now both burst into sobs of terror. 'We're going to be burnt! Nurse, nurse, let us out; we will be good!'

They were hushed up in scorn by Douglas; but Molly soothed and comforted them, assuring them it was only a make-up, and that the house never would catch fire.

'And if it did catch fire I would get out safe,' said Betty solemnly; 'for I should climb out of the window and walk along the gutter, holding on by the roof; and then I should climb down by the pear tree over Uncle Harry's bedroom.'

'You couldn't do it,' said Douglas scoffingly; 'girls can't climb!'

'I could do it; I could do it now!'

'Then do it, do it; I dare you to do it!'

Betty's eyes sparkled; and Molly at once left the twins, and ran to the window and put her head out.

'I think she could do it if we lifted her out; but it looks awful dangerous; I should be afraid.'

'I'm not a bit afraid,' said Betty sturdily.

'You wait till you're once out. I dare you to do it!' And Douglas danced up and down in delight at the coming excitement.

Not a doubt entered Betty's head as to the right or wrong of such an escapade; her impulsive little soul was longing to prove to her brother her ability in climbing, and audacious as she was in daring feats, this seemed to be a test of her powers. The garret window was opened; it was in the roof, so Betty had no difficulty in climbing out and standing in the gutter, which ran right round the house. Then slowly and carefully, in sight of the four admiring faces at the window, she commenced her perilous walk. Steadying herself by leaning with one hand on the sloping roof at her right, Betty walked triumphantly on till she reached the corner of the house; here she hesitated.

'Come back,' called out Molly; 'you can't turn the corner!'

'I dare you to go on!' naughty Douglas cried excitedly.

There was breathless silence; but others besides the little inmates of the garret were watching this feat in horror. Two gentlemen were walking leisurely through the meadow in front of the house.

'What on earth is that on the roof, Stuart? Not a child, surely!'

'A child it is; good heavens! It's one of my hopeful nieces; she'll be dashed to pieces to a certainty! Come on, St. Clair; only don't make a row!'

They reached the house as Betty was in the act of turning the corner. For a moment the little figure swayed outwardly, and Captain Stuart quite expected that moment to be Betty's last; but she recovered her balance most miraculously, accomplished the turn successfully, and went steadily on till she reached the pear tree.

Both gentlemen remained perfectly silent, knowing that a start might produce a false step, and they watched her descent to the ground now with less anxiety. Half-way down had Betty got, when there was a rushing sound of feet, and nurse, with a scream of horror appeared on the scene.

Betty's nerves gave way; she placed her foot on a rotten branch, which broke under her; her hands relaxed their hold. Another scream from nurse, echoed by Mrs. Giles behind her, and the child fell heavily, but safely, into her uncle's arms below.

CHAPTER XII

UNCLE HARRY'S FRIEND

'There's a pretty welcome for a tired man who wants his dinner!'

Betty was standing before her uncle with a white little face and determined, set mouth, and nurse was releasing the other little prisoners and bringing them down to their uncle.

Captain Stuart's friend was lounging on the low window-seat of the best parlour, looking on with an amused eye.

'Nurse thinks you ought to have a good whipping,' continued Captain Stuart, stroking his long, fair moustache very gravely, though there was a twinkle in his blue eyes. 'I think we must have a court-martial first. Were you trying to kill yourself, Betty?'

'I was trying to save myself from a fire—I mean a fire that might be.'

The sentence was begun bravely, but the little lips began to quiver. Shaken by her fall, afraid of her uncle's anger, and uncomfortable by the presence of a stranger, she burst into tears.

And then Captain Stuart took her on his knee, and drew out his large handkerchief.

'There, little woman, rest your head against my shoulder and cry away; it will do you good. I was beginning to think you a little stoic.'

The door opened, and the other children appeared, with very large eyes and solemn faces.

They kissed their uncle in a subdued fashion, and then Molly said, 'Nurse told us Betty had fallen, is she hurt?'

'Is her legs bwoken?' demanded the twins.

'I knew she couldn't do it; I told her she couldn't!'

In an instant Betty's face appeared from behind her handkerchief. 'I did do it; I did! and I could do it again to-morrow; so there, Douglas!'

Then Uncle Harry laughed outright, after which he pulled himself up, and said as sternly as he could,—

'Now look here, youngsters, I'm not good at scolding, as you know; but you're all old enough to know that it is not true pluck to go crawling round roofs like cats, and running the risks of breaking your necks and damaging your limbs for the rest of your lives. Now then, who is to blame? Speak up like little Britons, and don't be ashamed of owning up and telling the truth about it.'

There was a pause. Douglas got very red in the face, but blurted out, 'I dared her to do it.'

'And I said I thought she could do it,' said Molly with tearful eyes; 'but I did ask her to come back at the corner.'

'And I dared her to go on,' added Douglas.

'And Bobby and me clapped our hands at her,' put in Billy eagerly, feeling anxious to share in the glory of the escapade.

'Do you think it a brave thing to urge another on to danger, when, perhaps, you would be afraid of taking their place yourself?'

It was Douglas who was addressed, and he hung his head in shame.

'But he was just getting out of the window to follow her, when nurse came up,' said Molly, in defence of her favourite brother.

'I didn't know boys were in the habit of following girls,' remarked Captain Stuart drily. 'I think doughty Douglas must have another name. Listen, my boy, and remember this to the end of your life. There were two young fellows came out to join our battalion in Egypt. We were ordered out one morning on a reconnaissance, and both these youngsters came with us. They were strong, fresh-faced young fellows, one especially; he was the heir to a big property at home, and had left his widow mother to come and earn a name for himself. I can see him now, with his sparkling eyes and merry laugh, as he rode on just in front of me with his chum. I won't give you children details, but we had a sharp bit of fighting that morning, and bullets were flying pretty freely. At the finish, when returning, having dispersed our enemy, we came across another party of them entrenched on a height. Orders were given to fire lying down, as they were skilled marksmen and had the advantage of the position. "Now then," whispered one of these young fellows to the other, "make your name; scale the hillside and storm their fort."

'"I would if I had my orders to," was the quick retort.

'"We're like rabbits in the underwood," the youngster went on. "Do those skulking fellows think we're afraid of showing ourselves? A good British cheer and a sight of our rifles would soon send them to the right-about. The poor old major is dead beat and wants a nap, or he wouldn't give such an order. Show yourself, Castleton; let them have a sight of your six foot six. What? *afraid*!"

'In an instant Johnny Castleton stood up in the full strength of his manhood, and the next moment his brains were scattered by a bullet, his dead body falling into the arms of the friend who was the cause of his death. Do you think he died the death of a hero, Betty? How do you think his friend felt, Douglas, when he had to write home and tell the widowed mother her boy would never come back to her? Do you know, the folly of his act so weighed upon his mind that he left the army, and when I last heard of him his friends were afraid that his reason was giving way. There now! I've made your faces solemn enough to satisfy nurse. And you will never dare your sisters to do foolhardy exploits again, will you, my boy? And you will never listen to him if he does, girls? Now my lecture is ended, and you can tell nurse to forgive you all. Where is Mrs. Giles? I wonder if she could put up my friend for a night or two.'

Captain Stuart put Betty down from his knee, and rose to his feet. He so seldom lectured the children that his words left a deep impression, and none of them ever forgot the lesson imprinted on their minds. They were rather subdued for the rest of the day, and not altogether pleased at the advent of Major St. Clair.

Amy Le Feuvre

'We shan't get Uncle Harry a bit to ourselves,' grumbled Douglas, as the children were playing in the garden whilst the gentlemen were at dinner; 'he'll be going out fishing with that other fellow every day, and he's going to stay the whole week with him.'

'I like him rather,' said Molly; 'he is something like Mr. Roper.'

'He has nice sad eyes,' put in Betty; 'and he likes Prince.'

But before long Major St. Clair was taken into favour. He was a tall, dark man, with rather a stern look, until he smiled; and then the children knew they need not be afraid, for he had more smiles than frowns for them during his stay. Douglas, to his great delight, was allowed to go fishing with them.

'You see,' he confided to his sisters, 'they couldn't get on very well without me, as I'm learning to put their bait on for them, and I help to unpack their luncheon-basket, and very often I lie down on the bank and tell them stories; they like that very much.'

One afternoon they were all in the orchard under some shady trees: the gentlemen were smoking and reading the papers, the children playing a little way off. Presently Betty came sauntering up to her uncle, Prince close at her heels.

'We're going for a walk,' she said; 'I s'pose you wouldn't like to come with us?'

None of the little Stuarts ever did anything without first inviting their uncle to participate in it.

'No, I wouldn't,' he said, leaning lazily back in his wicker chair and surveying the little figure before him with amused eyes. 'Where are you bound? Your independence of thought and action will be sadly crippled when you get back to town. Does nurse let you all scour the country at your own free will?'

'What does scour mean?' asked Betty with knitted brows. 'Does it mean scrub? for I'm sure the country doesn't want cleaning.' Then, not liking the laugh following her words, she went on hastily: 'Nurse doesn't ask where I go, so I don't tell her; but I go to church, when I don't go to Mr. Russell.'

'And what do you do there?'

'Well,' said Betty, looking very steadily at her uncle, 'if you and Major St. Clair won't say anything about it, I'll tell you.'

'Wild horses won't tear it from me,' said the major.

'I go to take some flowers to a little dead girl there; she likes to smell them, and hold them in her hands instead of the dead lily she has got. And then I've got a friend who meets me there—a lady she is—and she sings the most beautiful songs on the organ! they make me cry sometimes. And the church is so dark, and still, and cool; it's a beautiful place.'

'Will you let me come with you?' asked Major St. Clair, rising as he spoke.

'It is an enchanting programme,' murmured Uncle Harry; 'tears amongst the dead! I warn you, my dear fellow, the church is nearly a mile away.'

'I want to stretch my legs,' was the response.

Betty set off radiant, with much self-importance.

'You see,' she said, looking up at the major through her long lashes as she trotted along at his side, 'I don't always ask people to come with me; Prince and I are quite enough. But you're a visitor, and so is Uncle Harry. You won't talk or make a noise in church, will you? And will you help me to get some honeysuckle from the hedge as we go along? Violet will like to smell it—at least, I make believe she will.'

The walk seemed a short one to the major, Betty entertained him so well. When they reached the church, she took him straight to the monument she loved so much, and was pleased with his genuine admiration of it. She placed the honeysuckle reverentially in the clasped hands of the little figure, which she stooped down to kiss as usual, and then pointed to the stained window above.

'Don't you like it?' she said in a solemn whisper. 'And do you see the text? Mr. Russell put it there. I was asking him the other day about it. I asked him if he was like one of the disciples that wanted to keep the children away from Jesus, and if he put it up for that, and he said, Yes, he did want to forbid Violet to go to Jesus when He called her. I expect Violet is very glad she wasn't kept back, don't you think so?'

'I expect so,' the major responded gravely.

'She wasn't any bigger than me,' continued Betty, standing before the window with clasped hands, and that upward dreamy look that always came upon her sweet little face when talking about serious things, 'but she's got through tribulation safely. Mr. Russell told me how she bore all the pain of her illness for a whole year without a grumble; and pain and suffering is tribulation, isn't it?'

'What do you know about tribulation?'

How often had Betty been asked that question!

'I know a great deal about it,' she said, looking at the major very earnestly; 'and though I haven't had it, I'm expecting to. Have you had it?'

'No, I don't know that I have,' was the amused reply. Then, a shadow crossing his face, he added: 'Trouble and I are not strangers. I think I have had my share.'

'And a big trouble is tribulation, isn't it? And it's on the way to heaven.'

Then the major smiled his sweet smile. 'That's it, Betty, on the way to heaven. We must through much tribulation enter into the kingdom of God.'

'And have you had a big trouble?' persisted the child.

'Yes, I have,' the major said slowly; 'a very big trouble, Betty. At one time of my life it would have overwhelmed me, but I've learnt to take things differently now.'

'You'll hear my friend sing about tribulation, p'raps, if I ask her to; she will be here directly. Where will you sit? I like to sit on the chancel step, and Prince sits in my lap.'

'I will find a seat for myself. Perhaps I shall slip away into the sunshine again.'

And Major St. Clair sauntered round the church, looking at the old tablets until he heard the door open, and then he slipped into a seat at the side of the church behind an old stone pillar.

Betty seated herself on the chancel steps after her greetings

Amy Le Feuvre

with her friend were over. The picture she made as she sat there was long riveted on Major St. Clair's memory: the golden sunshine streaming in, the old carved pews in the background, and the dainty little white figure hugging her spaniel in her arms, would have charmed an artist's eye. But it was not this sight that made the strong man suddenly turn pale and clutch the back of the seat in front of him with nervous, trembling hands; his startled gaze was no longer upon Betty, but upon the slight, graceful figure that was now taking her seat at the organ.

Betty's clear, childish voice was heard,—

'Please sing about tribulation. I've brought some one with me who would like to hear it. He's listening at the back of the church.'

Nesta gave a hasty look round, but seeing no one, turned again to the organ, and in a minute her beautiful voice rose in the triumphant strains of the song of the redeemed. Major St. Clair folded his arms, and stood up behind his pillar. He seemed strangely moved, and as the last notes died away he hastily quitted the church.

CHAPTER XIII

'WHEN WE TWO MET!'

Betty was so absorbed in the music that she forgot all about the major.

'When I grow up, do you think I shall be able to play and sing like you do?' she asked, with a little sigh of happiness.

'I dare say you may, dear.'

'But shall I have an organ to play? In London you can't go into any church and play, can you?'

'No; it is only because I know the clergyman here that he gives me permission.'

'And why do you never come to church here on Sunday?'

'Because we have a little church nearer us; but it has not an organ, and so I come over here.'

'Do you know what I do when you're singing? I shut my eyes and pretend I'm in heaven. It's lovely! If you shut yours you could pretend too, and I wish you could go on singing for ever and ever!'

Nesta laughed, and kissed the little eager, up-turned face. 'I should get very tired and hungry, I'm afraid. I am not an angel, Betty; but you're right, darling. I, too, get very near to heaven when I'm singing;' and she added musingly,—

In heart and mind ascending,
My spirit follows Thee.'

When, a little later, Nesta came out of the church with Betty, the tall figure of Major St. Clair came forward to meet them.

'Good-afternoon, Miss Fairfax.'

His tone was cold and grave; but Nesta started, and turned white to her very lips; then with an effort she recovered her composure, and held out her hand.

'It is a long time since we have met,' she said.

There was a pause, but Betty came to the rescue with the delightful unconsciousness of childhood.

'Do you know my Miss Fairfax?' she asked the major. 'You never told me you did. Didn't she sing beautifully? Did you like "Tribulation"? We like it the best of all her songs, don't we, Prince?'

She stooped to caress her little dog; then, as he broke away from her, she darted after him.

Major St. Clair stood still, and his eyes never moved from Nesta's face.

'Do we meet as strangers?' he asked.

'No,' she said, a little unsteadily, and her lips quivered in spite of herself, as she strove in vain to meet his gaze calmly; 'as old friends, I hope.'

'Never!' he said, a passionate light coming to his eyes; 'it must be everything or nothing to me, as I told you long ago.'

She was silent; a little sigh escaped her, so hopeless and yet so patient, that Major St. Clair continued hotly,—

'I would not have come here, had I known you were in this neighbourhood; but having met I cannot go without a word with you. Nesta, you are not happy; I see it in your face! Time has not soothed and comforted you; why will you not let me share your trouble and stand by you when perhaps you need a friend more than ever you did in days of old? Do you realize the blank you are making in my life, as well as in your own? Yes, I know I am taking much for granted; but yours is not a nature to change. I believe in you now as I always did, and it is only your mistaken ideas of duty that have brought this trouble into our lives.'

He paused, and then Nesta spoke, looking away from the low churchyard wall by which they were standing to the hills in the distance.

'I am sorry we have met,' she said simply, 'very sorry, for it is pain to us both; but the circumstances in my life have not changed; I cannot act differently; my mother and sister require me, and my mother—' Her voice faltered.

'Your mother is still of the same opinion,' he said. 'I look back with regret to my heated words when last I saw her. Time and another Teacher has shown me since where I was wrong; but, Nesta, let me plead my—may I say our cause with her again? She has no right to spoil our lives, and it is no true kindness to her to allow her to do it. Give me your permission to come and see her.'

'I cannot; it will only stir up her grief and pain afresh. She will not, cannot, look at things in a different light.'

'And are you going to part with me like this?'

His tone was low and husky with feeling. He added, a little drearily, 'I wonder, after all, if your affection has cooled; you speak so calmly about it all, that it makes one think—'

Nesta heard him so far, and then put out her hand as if to stop him.

'Oh, Godfrey!'

That was all; but as the old familiar name slipped from her lips she burst into tears, and turning aside, leant her arms on the old wall and buried her head in them.

Major St. Clair stepped up quickly. 'Nesta, Nesta, you must not! I cannot stand it! My darling, we cannot part like this!'

What he might have done was never known; perhaps, with his strong arm round her, Nesta would have yielded then and there; but a most inopportune childish voice broke in close by.

'You've made her cry! You've made my Miss Fairfax cry!' And with a little rush Betty flew to comfort her friend.

In an instant Nesta was standing erect again.

'It is nothing, darling; we have been talking over old times. Good-bye, Major St. Clair.'

She turned down a path at the side of the church, whilst Major St. Clair gazed after her in bewilderment and vexation.

'Oh!' he said, shaking his head at Betty as they retraced their way homewards, 'you're like a little boy I once knew, who would bring me a delicious plate of cherries. "Would you like to have some, major? Look at them; aren't they lovely?" And then, as I stretched out my hand, he would snatch them back with malicious glee, and gobble them up in my sight.'

'He was a very rude little boy,' said Betty, a little offended, 'and I don't think I'm a bit like him, for I haven't brought you anything this afternoon.'

Very restless and uneasy was Major St. Clair all that evening; Captain Stuart more than once took him to task for his moodiness and absence of mind, but was quite unsuccessful in eliciting a satisfactory explanation.

The next day they went off fishing together, but about four o'clock Major St. Clair left his friend and sauntered back to the house. Finding Betty and Prince playing together outside, he called her to him, and, lying full length on the grass, led her on to talk about Nesta. Betty innocently fell in with his wish; she gave him a graphic description of her day at Holly Grange, and then went back to the day when she first met Mrs. Fairfax in the wood.

'She's like a queen,' said the eager child; 'her face is so stern and proud, but she's very sad! Every grown-up person seems sad about here! I like Mrs. Fairfax very much; she gave me Prince.'

Major St. Clair listened, and asked questions, and then suddenly started to his feet.

'Come for a walk with me,' he said; 'wait till I have written a letter, and then we will start.'

'To church again?' inquired Betty.

'No, not to church; to Holly Grange.'

'It's miles and miles,' said Betty dubiously; 'I went in a pony carriage, but if you go by the wood it is shorter.'

'Oh, we shall manage it very well, and if you are tired I will carry you.'

Major St. Clair's tone was quite cheerful, and Betty set off with him, delighted at being chosen as his companion.

'Are you going to see Miss Fairfax?' she asked presently.

'No, I don't think I shall go into the house at all; but I want you to take a note to Mrs. Fairfax and bring me back an answer.'

Betty coloured up with pleasure. 'I shall like to do that,' she said; 'it's such a nice house inside, and you should see the flowers! I think I could be quite happy if I were Mrs. Fairfax, couldn't you?'

She chattered on, and when at last the gates were reached, Major St. Clair entrusted her with the important letter.

'Give it to Mrs. Fairfax yourself, Betty, and tell her I would like to see her very much.'

Betty nodded, and clasped the letter tightly in one little hand, Prince followed her closely up the drive. The hall-door stood open, and for a moment the child hesitated; then the old butler crossed the hall, and she called out eagerly,—

'Please, can I come in and see Mrs. Fairfax?'

The man looked surprised. 'I don't think she will see you,' he said, smiling; 'Mrs. Fairfax sees no visitors.'

'But I'm not a visitor,' said the little girl; 'I'm only Betty, and I've got a letter to give her.'

'I will go and see.'

He disappeared, but returned a minute after.

'Come in, missy—this way.'

He led the child into the drawing-room, where Mrs. Fairfax was presiding at the afternoon tea-table. Nesta was not there, and Grace was just leaving the room.

A smile lightened Mrs. Fairfax's grave face at the sight of Betty.

'All alone?' she asked, bending down to kiss her.

'I've come to bring you a letter,' said Betty, dimpling over with pleasure and importance.

Mrs. Fairfax made her sit down in a little cushioned chair, and took the note in her hand. As she read it, she knitted her brows, and her lips took their sternest curve; then rising she went to the farther end of the room, and stood looking out of the low French window, her back turned to Betty, and her hands clenched convulsively by her side.

Nesta was right in surmising what a torrent of painful

Amy Le Feuvre

memories would be aroused by Major St. Clair's advent in their neighbourhood.

If the letter had come a few weeks before, there would have been only one answer; but Mrs. Fairfax had been learning lately from the great Master Himself, and her heart was softened and subdued. Still it was a hard struggle, and pride fought for predominance. At length she turned round, and went to her writing-desk; and then Betty crept up softly to her.

'Major St. Clair asked me to ask you to see him,' she said, laying her little hand on Mrs. Fairfax's knee.

'I will write my answer, Betty; I cannot do that,' was the cold reply, as Mrs. Fairfax turned her head away from the child.

But Betty was not to be put off.

'I think he would like to see you very much; and you'd like him, for he is Uncle Harry's friend; and he has such sad eyes, and he has been through tribulation like you; at least, he has had a big trouble, he told me; and that's just the same, isn't it?'

There was no answer. Betty continued: 'Shall I just go out and bring him in? I've been telling him about you this afternoon, and how you gave me the lilies, and Prince, and he liked to hear it; he asked me a lot of questions, and I think he wants to see you, and if you're like a queen, like I told him!'

Then Mrs. Fairfax lifted the child on her knee. 'Oh Betty, Betty!' was all she said, but some glistening drops fell on the child's curly head, as the grey head was bent over it, and Betty wondered why Mrs. Fairfax's voice sounded so strange. 'I think you will have to bring him in here,' Mrs. Fairfax said at last; and Betty trotted out of the room in great delight. She found the major pacing up and down the road with a white, resolute face. He threw away the cigar he was smoking when he saw the child, and asked, with anxiety in his dark eyes,—

'Well, little woman, how have you fared?'

'You're to come in and see her.'

'Thank God!' and not another word did the major say till he was in the drawing-room.

It was a constrained and formal greeting between the two; and then Mrs. Fairfax turned to Betty,—

'Will you run into the garden, dear, till we call you? I think Grace is out there.'

Betty obeyed. Grace was walking slowly up and down the path, enveloped in shawls, and did not look well-pleased when the childish voice sounded in her ear,—

'May I come and walk with you?'

'Were you sent out here? Nesta, I suppose, as usual is out, so she will not be able to look after you, and I certainly am not in a fit state of health to amuse you and keep you out of mischief.'

'I'm not going to get into mischief, really,' protested Betty in an aggrieved tone; 'I'll walk quietly along with you, and won't even pick a flower. Are you better today?'

'No, I am not better—I don't expect I ever shall be, though I can get no sympathy from any one in this house.'

'What's the matter with you?' asked Betty.

'Now, if you are going to worry me with questions, you can just run away; if you were to be kept awake night after night, and never know what it was to be without headaches, having every nerve in your body quivering from exhaustion, you wouldn't wonder what the matter was.'

'I expect you're like Violet, only she could never leave her bed. Mr. Russell said she would sometimes have no sleep all night, and she was so patient, she used to say, "Read me about there shall be no pain." Mr. Russell said he wouldn't have been half so patient as she was. And now she is singing right in the middle of "these are they which came out of great tribulation." Wouldn't you like to be her?'

Grace was silent. Betty's active little tongue turned to other subjects; she told about her visit to the Hall, of her 'dead figure' which was being made out of 'soft putty'; of Prince's misdemeanours when he tried to chase chickens, and then came back to his little mistress with his tail between his legs; of Douglas and Molly's wonderful games, and the twins' talents for getting into trouble; she told her of her walk on the roof, and the story of the young soldiers related by Uncle Harry; and Grace listened, and eventually was amused and interested in spite of herself.

It was a long time before Betty was summoned to the house; and then she met the major in the hall.

'Run in, little one, and wish Mrs. Fairfax good-bye.'

Mrs. Fairfax stooped to kiss Betty; all the hard lines in her face had disappeared, and her voice was unusually gentle.

'You must come and see me another day, when I have no business to occupy me.'

And Betty put her arms round her neck, and gave her a delighted hug.

'You will meet Nesta coming back from the church if you keep to the lane,' Mrs. Fairfax said, speaking to Major St. Clair; 'and we shall expect you to dinner tomorrow.'

He raised his hat, and strode round the shrubbery with such energy that it was all Betty could do to keep up with him.

'Don't you think Mrs. Fairfax like a queen?' asked Betty presently. 'Was she like what I told you?'

'I have seen Mrs. Fairfax before,' was the major's short reply; and Betty gave a little disappointed 'Oh!'

Not long afterwards they came in sight of Nesta. She was walking along rather slowly, her eyes and her thoughts far away; but when she saw who it was, a quick colour spread over her face.

Major St. Clair stepped forward quickly.

'Your mother has sent me to you,' he said; and there was a glad ring in his tone. Nesta looked up at him bewildered.

'My mother! Have you seen her?'

'Yes; thanks to this little person here with me.'

Betty was kissed, but for once Nesta seemed oblivious of her presence. The child could not understand it, neither could she understand the explanation that followed in low, earnest tones. She saw Nesta's eyes light up with a sudden joy, and then fill with tears; she saw Major St. Clair bend his head very close to hers, and though she stood silently by she might just as well have been miles away, for all the notice that she received. At last with a little sigh she said,—

'I'm rather tired; I think I'll go home with Prince.'

Nesta turned to her at once.

'You poor little mite! Godfrey, will you carry her? I must leave you. No, don't come with me. I shall see you to-morrow, and I would rather see my mother alone. She has been so different lately, but I never dared to hope for this! Good-bye, Betty; you have been our little benefactor.'

Betty was hoisted on the broad shoulders of the major, and carried home in silence; he was busy with his own thoughts, and she was tired and sleepy.

They found Captain Stuart impatiently waiting for dinner.

'Where have you been?' he asked; 'has Betty bewitched you?'

'She has done me a good turn to-day,' responded the major.

Betty dipped her little hand into her uncle's.

'We've been to Holly Grange, Uncle Harry. I think Major St. Clair and my Miss Fairfax must have quarrelled yesterday, for he made her cry; but they kissed each other and made it up to-day, and now we're all friends.'

CHAPTER XIV

A HERO'S DEATH

Captain Stuart's week was prolonged to a fortnight, much to the children's delight. They were all astonished when they heard that Major St. Clair was going to marry Betty's Miss Fairfax. Betty herself was very puzzled about it, for she was still unconscious of how large a part she had played in the little drama; and only wondered sometimes that Nesta seemed to care so little for the organ now, and was so often occupied in walking or driving with the major. This, perhaps, made her enjoy her visits to Mr. Russell's studio the more; and when one day he put the finishing touch to the bit of sculpture, she looked rather wistfully at him.

'And mustn't I come here any more now?'

'Come as often as you like,' was the hearty reply; 'I like you chatting away to me whilst I work.'

'I've a good many friends here,' announced Betty upon the last evening of Captain Stuart's stay; 'I think I've more friends than Molly and Douglas have. They don't care about grown-up people: I rather like them!'

'We like Uncle Harry,' protested Molly.

'And who do you like the best of all your friends, Betty?' asked Major St. Clair.

'I think I like Mr. Russell. You see, he's an odd one, like I used to be before I had Prince. Miss Fairfax used to be an odd one too, but she's one of a couple now. Mr. Russell has got no one; he's quite alone.'

There was great laughter at Betty's speech.

'I think I'm an odd one, Betty,' Captain Stuart said. 'What do you advise? My making myself into a couple?'

'Two and two are so much more comfortable,' went on Betty gravely; 'I don't really know what I should do if I hadn't Prince to go with! Really at the bottom of my heart I love him better than anybody! Couldn't you get a dog, if you can't get any one else, Uncle Harry? You'd find yourself in a very nice couple then.'

How Captain Stuart laughed! And Betty was the only one who could see no joke in the matter.

After the gentlemen had left, the children had a quiet time. Betty would still steal away to the church to hear Nesta sing and play; and one day all the children spent a day at Holly Grange. Nurse was getting a little tired of the quiet country life, and began to talk about the return to London, which filled her little charges' hearts with dismay.

'It will be dreadful to sit up and do lessons again,' moaned Molly.

'I think,' said Douglas slowly, 'that I shall get lost the day we are going back; and then I shall live in the wood in that little hut; I shall be a kind of wild man; and I shall eat berries and nuts, and when I want some meat I shall kill a rabbit, and cook him! I really cannot stand being cooped up in that nursery at home again.'

'I've never, never been so happy in my life before,' Betty chimed in; 'but then of course I shall take Prince with me. Fancy! If we had never come to this farm, we should never have gone to that wood, and I should never have seen Mrs. Fairfax, and she would have never sent me Prince!'

'It's always "Prince" with you,' Douglas said a little impatiently; 'you can talk of no one else.'

The day following the one on which this conversation was held, Farmer Giles came into the kitchen in great perturbation about twelve o'clock.

'Where are the children?' he demanded quickly.

Nurse came into the room, leading Bobby, who had been undergoing a change of garments through a tumble into the duck-pond.

'They're out in the meadows,' she said; 'what's the matter?'

'I'm afraid there's a dog of Mr. Dart's loose; I've just heard say it's gone mad, and can't be found! It's these dreadful hot days. I've just chained up Rough. Little Miss Betty must look after that dog of hers. Tom Dart and a neighbour is out huntin' for theirs now.'

'A mad dog!' exclaimed nurse in horror; 'call them in, Jack, do! What should I do if they met it?'

And leaving Bobby in the kitchen, she as well as her brother ran out to warn the children. They found them in a clover field under the trees: Douglas was busy trying to work his way inside an old hollow trunk; Molly was digging down a rabbit hole; and Billy was waiting upon them both.

'Where is Miss Betty?'

'She's gone along the lane,' said Douglas, looking up with a very heated face; 'I sent her to the brook to get some water: we're going to lay in provisions for a siege; and this tree will be our hiding-place.'

'And I'm digging for treasure money,' said Molly.

'Is Prince with her?' asked nurse anxiously.

'Yes, he won't ever stay with us.'

'They're safe enough in this field,' said Farmer Giles, looking round; 'but they'd best not wander in the lanes. We must have Miss Betty back.'

Betty meanwhile was trotting contentedly along, hugging an old earthenware jar.

'We'll get them some water, Prince, and then you shall be the sentry; Douglas said you could be; directly you hear a step you must bark!'

Prince looked up, wagged his tail in response, and began to burrow in the grass for imaginary frogs.

And then Betty, feeling her jar very heavy, sat down against the hedge bank to rest. She remained there some time, chattering away to her dog, and was just starting on her way again, when shouts up the lane startled her.

A moment after, and straight down the lane towards her tore a large retriever; his mouth was open and covered with foam, and he kept making snaps at the air as he rushed along. After him came two men and some boys.

'Out of the way!' they shouted; 'he's mad!'

Poor little Betty stood in the middle of the lane, quite petrified. It was a very narrow lane; the banks and hedges were high on either side, and there literally seemed no escape for the child. On he came, with open jaws and bloodshot eyes; and in another moment a shrill childish scream rose in the air, which sent an awful chill through nurse's blood; for she was now close upon the scene. She arrived just as Tom Dart had got near enough to the dog to fire, and the report of a gun went off as she clambered over a gate into the lane.

She saw the body of the poor beast in the road, with Tom standing over it, but with trembling limbs made her way along to the little crowd now assembled higher up the lane. They were bending down over something in the middle of the road. Was it Betty?

'Is she safe? Who is hurt?' she gasped, as she pushed her way through. There, in agony of grief and terror, Betty was sitting upon the ground, shielding with her little arms her precious dog. 'You shan't take him from me, you shan't; he's my very own, and he's nearly killed!' she was crying frantically.

Nurse seized hold of her and the dog together. 'Are you hurt, child? Speak! Thank God, it's only the dog!'

Farmer Giles was already there, questioning the excited crowd. 'He was making straight for her, but the little dog dashed in front just in time. See how he's bitten! Take him away from the little missy; he'll have to be shot! 'Twas lucky for her she had him with her!' This and more was told, with gaps and pauses; but Betty saw and heard nothing of what was going on around her. She seemed almost beside herself with terror and grief.

'Take us away, nurse! Get a doctor! he's bleeding! He mustn't, oh, he mustn't die! Don't touch him! Oh, I won't, I won't let him go!'

'Come, come,' said Farmer Giles soothingly; 'I won't hurt him. We must see where he is bitten; perhaps I can put him to rights. You let me carry him home. There, see, he's been bitten in his neck, but you're hurting him, holding him so tightly! You let me carry him for you, and you can walk by my side.'

'Will you bathe him, and put a bandage round, and make him well again?'

There was hope dawning in the blue eye raised so trustfully to his; and for a moment the farmer hesitated; then he said, 'We'll do the best for him we can.'

And Betty opened her arms, and Prince was tenderly lifted up, and a piece of sacking the farmer happened to have with him was wrapped round him. He lifted his head, and tried to lick Betty's little hands as he was being taken from her; and she with a fresh burst of sobbing got up from the ground, and clutching hold of the farmer's coat, walked back to the house with him, nurse trying in vain to comfort her.

Arrived at the farm, nurse took decided measures, 'You come indoors with me, there's a good child; and let Jack attend to Prince. He will come and tell you when he's better. No, I won't let you take him in your arms again—now I mean it.'

'I must just see him once more; I must, nurse!'

'Ay,' said the farmer, giving nurse a peculiar look, 'she shall have one more look at him, before I take him!'

The sacking was uncovered, and Prince's ears pricked up and his bright brown eyes sought his little mistress's face. Betty bent over him, and was allowed to kiss the back of his brown silky head. 'My little darling,' she whispered, though tears began to fall again; 'I wish I had been bitten instead of you!' Then turning to Farmer Giles, she said, clasping her little hands in agony of entreaty,—

'You'll be as quick as ever you can, won't you? You won't be more than five minutes bathing his neck and binding it up, will you? and then I'll sit by and nurse him till he gets better. Will you put him in this basket and bring him to me as soon as ever you can?'

'Yes, yes,' said the farmer a little gruffly, and then he went out to the stables; and Betty stood by the kitchen window, too well trained in obedience to attempt to follow him, but with her little heart overflowing with longing to have Prince in her arms again.

'Now,' said nurse very kindly but determinedly, 'come up into the nursery, and let me wash your face and hands and put you on a clean pinafore.'

'He will get better, won't he, nurse? He didn't look very hurt. Can I give him some bread and milk when Farmer Giles brings him in?'

Nurse evaded this question; she seemed ill at ease; and when a few minutes afterwards the report of a gun went off, she started violently, then gave a sigh of relief. Betty was too absorbed in her own thoughts to notice this; and, directly her toilet was finished, she ran downstairs to the kitchen again.

'Has Prince come in, Mrs. Giles? Is he better?'

'Bless your little heart,' said Mrs. Giles, bustling about, 'Jack will be in directly, and he'll tell you.'

And, a few minutes afterwards, Farmer Giles appeared. Betty ran to him with outstretched hands. 'Where is he? Are you going to take me to him?'

The farmer looked helplessly at his wife.

'Where is nurse?' he said.

'Keeping out of the way,' muttered Mrs. Giles.

The farmer fetched a deep breath. 'Come along, then,' he said; 'I've done my best, and mustn't shirk the consequence.'

He took hold of Betty's hand, and led her to the stables; twice he cleared his throat, as if about to speak, and then at the door, keeping one hand on the latch, he put his other one under Betty's little chin and raised her face.

'You'll be a brave, good little maid, won't you?' he said, 'and you'll bear up, for 'tis better for the little dog than to live in suffering.'

He opened the door, and Betty, not in the slightest understanding his words, pushed her way breathlessly in.

There in his basket, cold and stiff, lay poor little Prince! For one minute Betty thought he was asleep, and then the awful truth dawned upon her. With her blue eyes dilating with horror, she turned and faced the old farmer, and every vestige of colour left her cheeks.

'He's not dead!' she cried. 'Wake him up, Mr. Giles; he shan't be dead!'

'My little maid, I'm dreadful sorry for you; but 'tis better so; and his neck were near bitten through; he couldn't have lived long in any case.'

Betty flung herself on the floor with such a sharp wail of despair that Farmer Giles felt a lump rising in his throat He knew there could be no comfort yet for the broken-hearted child; that she must go through her trouble alone—words at such a time were useless; and after watching her for some minutes, he slipped away to fetch nurse to bring her in.

And Betty lay with her arms round Prince's basket, sobbing her very heart out, and feeling as if light and joy and gladness had gone out of her life for ever! When nurse came in a little later, and put a gentle hand on the little crouching figure, Betty turned round, furious in her grief.

'Go away, I shan't leave Prince; I wish I could die! Oh, nurse, nurse!' and a fresh burst of sobs shook her; 'tell me he isn't dead; tell me he isn't!'

Nurse tried in vain to pacify her; Betty was too over-wrought to listen. One thing she stedfastly refused to do, and that was to leave her dog, and nurse finally had to take her up in her arms by force, and carry her, shrieking and struggling, to the house. Poor little Betty did not prove herself a heroine; but nurse made allowance for her, and was unusually patient and tender.

'It's like a bit of her life gone,' she confided to Mrs. Giles. 'I always think it a pity when children get so wrapped up with their pets, but Miss Betty never does anything by halves.'

All that hot afternoon Betty lay on her bed in the nursery. Nurse could not tempt her to eat any dinner; and when the first paroxysm of grief was over, she lay there, white and silent, with little clenched hands, and now and then a quick-drawn sob escaping her.

Nurse was relieved and thankful when, going in quietly shortly before tea-time, she found her fast asleep, utterly worn out by her trouble.

CHAPTER XV

COMFORTED

Betty did not wake before the children's bedtime, and nurse did not disturb her; she trusted that a long night's rest would do her good.

But early the next morning the awakening came, and with it an undefined sense of misery. The little hand was at once put out for Prince's basket.

'Prince, wake up, darling!'

There was no basket! What had happened? Was it all an ugly dream? But where was Prince?

And then Molly woke by feeling a tugging at her bedclothes, and there was Betty, with round frightened eyes, standing over her.

'Molly, Molly, wake up; tell me it is only a dream! Where is Prince?'

Molly sat up, rubbed her eyes, and tried to recover her lost senses; then she looked sorrowfully at her little sister.

'Don't you remember, Betty? You get into bed with me, and I'll tell you again. Nurse told us all about it; and me and Douglas are dreadfully sorry too!'

Betty crept into Molly's bed, with much heart-sinking; the bad dream was truth then, and Prince was dead!

'Douglas and I went to see him in the stable,' Molly continued in a whisper. 'Farmer Giles said he saved your life; so he was quite a hero, Betty. Don't you think he ought to have a tombstone telling about it? Douglas wondered if you would go into mourning for him; but I don't think people wear black for dogs, do they?'

'He saved my life,' murmured Betty; 'oh, why did he? I wish I'd died instead; if Prince is dead, I can't live!' And then, with a fresh burst of tears, she sobbed, 'And I shall be the odd one again! I shall always be left out! and I shan't be in a couple any more! And, oh! I must see Prince again; dear darling Prince, he was the only friend I've ever had.' Then, drying her tears, she sat up. 'I'm going to the stable to look at him once again, Molly. I must give him a real good-bye kiss; I couldn't yesterday.'

'But he's buried,' Molly put in quickly. 'After tea last night we had his funeral. Farmer Giles dug a grave for him under our nice old apple tree in the orchard, he said it was best to get him out of your sight.'

This was a terrible blow to Betty. 'I think I might have been at his funeral; he was my dog, and you and Douglas didn't care for him a bit! Farmer Giles is a horrid man! But, oh dear, oh dear, I don't care for anything now he's dead!'

And the curly head sank back on the pillow; and, like Ahab of old, Betty turned her face to the wall and refused to be comforted.

For the next few days Betty gave nurse much anxiety; she crept about with a white face and flagging footsteps, refused to play with the other children, and spent most of her time sitting by Prince's grave. She had no appetite, and had restless, wakeful nights.

'Fretting herself ill over it,' was Mrs. Giles's comment; 'she'll be better when she gets back to London.'

Nesta Fairfax came down to see her little favourite, and Betty shed many tears on her knee.

'It's no good; I shall never, never be happy again! No one cares for me like Prince; and now he's dead I've no friend left!'

'You have a good many friends, Betty. Listen, darling; when I'm married I'm going to live in London, and you shall come and stay with me sometimes, if your mother will allow it.'

'When are you going to be married?'

'Soon; but we shall have a very quiet wedding, or I would have you as a little bridesmaid.'

Betty shook her curly head mournfully. 'It's no good, my heart is broken; and I don't want to stay with anybody or do anything.'

She had the same answer to any one who tried to comfort her. And then one afternoon Mr. Russell appeared on the scene. When he heard from nurse how matters lay, he proposed that Betty should come and stay with him for a week. 'It is change of scene and atmosphere that she wants.

Let me take her back with me at once; my housekeeper will take good care of her.' And this was managed, and Betty walked away with him quietly and contentedly.

She was certainly happier roaming through his big house than she had been at the farm; but there seemed to be some extra weight on her mind that she would not reveal, and it was not until the first Sunday after her arrival there that he discovered the cause.

They had been to church together, had waited until the congergation had dispersed, and stood by Violet's monument. Betty had placed some fresh roses on it, and as they were leaving the church she said, looking back wistfully,—

'I wish Prince had been buried in church; no one cares about his grave! I put flowers on it, but the chickens run through the orchard and scratch them off; and one day the horrid black pig was grunting with his nose, and making a great hole in it! I wish he could have a tombstone; no one cares a bit, and they almost laugh if I say anything about it.'

'Is that what is troubling you?' asked Mr. Russell kindly.

'That's one of the things, but not the big thing.'

'And what is the big thing?'

Betty was silent; then she said, 'I'll tell it to you—p'raps this afternoon.'

They went back to luncheon, and then Mr. Russell took his seat in the shady verandah that ran round the house. It was a still, warm afternoon. Betty got a stool, and sitting down on it rested her head against the knee of her friend. Outside the bees were humming round the roses and amongst the bright flower-beds on the lawn; the birds were twittering in the old beeches close by; but over the whole scene hung a Sabbath peace and repose.

The child looked away to the soft distant hills and the deep blue sky.

'Shall I tell you what I promised?' she asked at last, bringing her sad little eyes to Mr. Russell's face.

Mr. Russell nodded, and clutching rather nervously at his hand, Betty said a little hurriedly, 'Prince has always been so good, and I've talked so much to him of heaven, and he seemed to like it, and I—well, I tried to teach him his prayers, and I've prayed to God for him every night, that I thought he would be sure to go to heaven, don't you think so? But I was reading Revelation, and I was thinking how perhaps he might be able to sing in heaven, perhaps God would give him a proper voice—for Mrs. Giles told me she had a little deaf and dumb brother once who died, and she said he would be given a voice when he got there; and then I read in the last chapter—oh, I can't tell you!'

Down dropped the little head, and a burst of tears came.

Mr. Russell did not speak; he got up and went inside the house to get a Bible. Coming back, he spread it open on his knee and scanned the chapter through.

'Well,' he said at length, 'I don't see your trouble, Betty.'

'It says,' sobbed the child, 'that dogs will be outside heaven with all the wicked persons and all the liars! Prince was never wicked, and never, never told a lie. I can't make it out, it's so dreadful!'

Mr. Russell almost smiled, but his tone was as grave as usual when he put his arm round Betty, saying, 'But, my dear child, that is not the meaning of the verse. How can I explain it to you? Let me try: the term dog was used by the Jews to express anything unclean, despicable; the Palestine dogs were wild, savage animals, despised and scouted by every one; and so people who led wicked lives, without any right feeling or principle, are compared to dogs.'

'Then it doesn't mean Prince? He may be in heaven after all? Oh, I wish I had asked some one about it, but I was afraid! Miss Fairfax said once he had no soul; but then I've asked God to give him one, and God can do anything, can't He? Do you think he is in heaven? Oh, Mr. Russell, he must be somewhere!'

The piteous tone went right to Mr. Russell's heart. He leant forward and lifted Betty on his knee.

'Betty, do you love God?'

'Yes.'

'Very much?'

'I think I do, and I feel He loves me.'

'I think you do too, for you have often talked to me about Him, and you have taught me to love Him too, Betty. Now you must trust God about Prince. I can't give you a text in the Bible to tell you Prince is in heaven, but God knows all about your little sorrowful heart. You tell him all about it, and be at rest. There are times when we go through life that we must do this, yes, grown-up men and women, Betty, when they cannot see, and struggle to understand and penetrate the unseen, are brought down under God's hand.

And He says to us, "I have done this: now is the time to trust Me." "Be still, and know that I am God." I have had to learn this lesson, and at times my heart has been hard and bitter. But there, why am I talking like this to you? You will not understand.'

'I like it,' said Betty, lying back in his arms, and looking out into the sunny garden. 'And I may think what I like about Prince now, mayn't I? I'm quite, quite sure God loves him. God loves everybody, even the wickedest sinners, and Prince wasn't a wicked dog at all.'

There was silence, which Betty broke at last.

'I like being here with you, because you talk to me so differently, and I feel so dreadfully alone at the farm. Nurse said you were a single gentleman, and your servants couldn't have much to do. I must be a single child, I feel! And they all say such stupid things to comfort me. Nurse said he would have had to die some time, and perhaps if I had taken him back to London he would have got run over, and Douglas said I must pretend I never had a dog called Prince; and Molly told me that Douglas will soon be going to school, and then she and I will be a couple; and Mrs. Giles said if Prince hadn't died he would have gone raving mad and bitten all of us, and made us raving mad too, and we would have all been shot, and we must be thankful; and Reuben, the old grave man, asked me if I didn't thank God that the mad dog didn't bite me; and old Jenny said perhaps I was making an idol of Prince, and so he was taken away. How could I make an idol of him? I wouldn't say my prayers to him instead of God! You wouldn't be comforted to have those things said to you, would you?'

'No, I don't think I should,' said Mr. Russell, smiling.

'Mrs. Fairfax wanted to give me another dog, a little puppy; but I couldn't, I couldn't have another dog when Prince is dead! You couldn't have another Violet, could you? I think you and I understand, because we've now both had some one dead belonging to us.'

Betty's week lengthened into three. Mr. Russell seemed loth to part with her, and her subdued spirits and pathetic grief touched him greatly. But the visit came to an end at last, and about four o'clock one bright afternoon the dog-cart was driven round to take her home, 'You shall come and see me again, Betty,' said Mr. Russell brightly, 'and I shall come and see you when I am in London. I used to be at Eton with your father, and shall like to renew his acquaintance. And next spring you ask your mother to take you to the Royal Academy, where all the pictures are. I think you will see a white statue of a little girl asleep on a log of wood, and a—' He stopped.

'And Prince,' put in Betty sadly. 'I shan't bear to look at him; and yet I should like to. I don't mind going back to London; I thought I could never be so happy anywhere as in the country, but I've been miserabler than I ever was in London. I shall be miserable now for ever and ever!'

'Betty,' said Mr. Russell suddenly, as they were driving through the sweet-scented lanes towards the farm-house, 'do you remember the text you said to me when I first saw you in the church, and you were putting forget-me-nots on my darling's tomb?'

'I expect it was my tribulation text,' said Betty musingly.

'Yes, it was. You told me you were unhappy because you had not been through tribulation, and a short time ago you told me that you were asking God to send you tribulation, and that you were hoping to get it soon.'

'And you told me the same as everybody else—that I didn't know what I was wishing for. But I did, and I expect God will answer it; for old Jenny said I should come through it, and perhaps I wouldn't have to wait till I grew up.'

'I think,' said Mr. Russell slowly, as he looked down at the wistful little face, 'that God has been answering your prayer already.'

Betty looked up breathlessly. 'How?'

'I think He has sent you a little bit of tribulation to see if you can bear it, and if you will be a good, patient child over it, and not keep saying you will never be happy again.'

Such a flash of light came across Betty's face, and into her big blue eyes.

'Do you really think God has taken away Prince to give me tribulation? Oh! Mr. Russell, is it true, could it be? Is this coming through tribulation?'

Her whole face was quivering with intense feeling.

'I think it is as big a trouble as a little child like you can be called upon to bear,' said Mr. Russell, drawing her close to him; 'and I think God has sent it to you for some good purpose.'

A long-drawn sigh came from the child, and not another word did she say; but when nurse and the other children came out to welcome her back, they were all surprised to see the radiant, happy look upon her face, and nurse inwardly congratulated herself upon the good her visit had done her.

Mr. Russell received a fervent kiss and hug on departing, and Betty came back to her own circle again.

But a glad surprise awaited her. Douglas and Molly were full of a suppressed mystery all tea-time; and, when it was over, they impatiently begged her to come to the orchard. She accompanied them willingly, but gave a cry of delight and astonishment when she reached the old apple tree. There was a neat little iron railing surrounding poor Prince's grave; above it was a stone pedestal, and upon this was lying the stone figure of Prince himself, the facsimile of the portrait of him lying at Betty's feet when she was fast asleep in the cornfield. Below in gold letters was written:—

'To THE MEMORY OF PRINCE,

Who gave his life for his mistress, 11th August, 18—.'

'Mr. Russell had it put up,' said Molly; 'he has come over several times about it, and he said he wanted it to be kept quite a secret till you came back. Isn't it lovely?'

But Betty had no voice to answer; tears were flowing freely, and when Douglas and Molly tried to comfort her, she assured them it was only because she was so happy. They left her there shortly after, and she stood silent for some time; then her little face shone again with a soft radiance, and kneeling down on the green grass, with closed eyes, she bent her curly head, and these were the words she uttered—

'O God, I thank You for answering my prayer, and sending me tribulation. I thank You that I'm in the text at last!'

THE END

Choose from Thousands of 1stWorldLibrary Classics By

Friedrich Kerst	Hayden Carruth	James Branch Cabell
Friedrich Nietzsche	Helent Hunt Jackson	James DeMille
Fyodor Dostoyevsky	Helen Nicolay	James Joyce
G.A. Henty	Hendrik Conscience	James Lane Allen
G.K. Chesterton	Hendy David Thoreau	James Lane Allen
Gabrielle E. Jackson	Henri Barbusse	James Oliver Curwood
Garrett P. Serviss	Henrik Ibsen	James Oppenheim
Gaston Leroux	Henry Adams	James Otis
George A. Warren	Henry Ford	James R. Driscoll
George Ade	Henry Frost	Jane Abbott
Geroge Bernard Shaw	Henry James	Jane Austen
George Cary Eggleston	Henry Jones Ford	Jane L. Stewart
George Durston	Henry Seton Merriman	Janet Aldridge
George Ebers	Henry W Longfellow	Jens Peter Jacobsen
George Eliot	Herbert A. Giles	Jerome K. Jerome
George Gissing	Herbert Carter	Jessie Graham Flower
George MacDonald	Herbert N. Casson	John Buchan
George Meredith	Herman Hesse	John Burroughs
George Orwell	Hildegard G. Frey	John Cournos
George Sylvester Viereck	Homer	John F. Kennedy
George Tucker	Honore De Balzac	John Gay
George W. Cable	Horace B. Day	John Glasworthy
George Wharton James	Horace Walpole	John Habberton
Gertrude Atherton	Horatio Alger Jr.	John Joy Bell
Gordon Casserly	Howard Pyle	John Kendrick Bangs
Grace E. King	Howard R. Garis	John Milton
Grace Gallatin	Hugh Lofting	John Philip Sousa
Grace Greenwood	Hugh Walpole	John Taintor Foote
Grant Allen	Humphry Ward	Jonas Lauritz Idemil Lie
Guillermo A. Sherwell	Ian Maclaren	Jonathan Swift
Gulielma Zollinger	Inez Haynes Gillmore	Joseph A. Altsheler
Gustav Flaubert	Irving Bacheller	Joseph Carey
H. A. Cody	Isabel Cecilia Williams	Joseph Conrad
H. B. Irving	Isabel Hornibrook	Joseph E. Badger Jr
H. C. Bailey	Israel Abrahams	Joseph Hergesheimer
H. G. Wells	Ivan Turgenev	Joseph Jacobs
H. H. Munro	J. G.Austin	Jules Vernes
H. Irving Hancock	J. Henri Fabre	Julian Hawthrone
H. R. Naylor	J. M. Barrie	Julie A Lippmann
H. Rider Haggard	J. M. Walsh	Justin Huntly McCarthy
H. W. C. Davis	J. Macdonald Oxley	Kakuzo Okakura
Haldeman Julius	J. R. Miller	Karle Wilson Baker
Hall Caine	J. S. Fletcher	Kate Chopin
Hamilton Wright Mabie	J. S. Knowles	Kenneth Grahame
Hans Christian Andersen	J. Storer Clouston	Kenneth McGaffey
Harold Avery	J. W. Duffield	Kate Langley Bosher
Harold McGrath	Jack London	Kate Langley Bosher
Harriet Beecher Stowe	Jacob Abbott	Katherine Cecil Thurston
Harry Castlemon	James Allen	Katherine Stokes
Harry Coghill	James Andrews	L. A. Abbot
Harry Houidini	James Baldwin	L. T. Meade

L. Frank Baum	Paul G. Tomlinson	T. S. Arthur
Latta Griswold	Paul Severing	The Princess Der Ling
Laura Dent Crane	Percy Brebner	Thomas A. Janvier
Laura Lee Hope	Percy Keese Fitzhugh	Thomas A Kempis
Laurence Housman	Peter B. Kyne	Thomas Anderton
Lawrence Beasley	Plato	Thomas Bailey Aldrich
Leo Tolstoy	Quincy Allen	Thomas Bulfinch
Leonid Andreyev	R. Derby Holmes	Thomas De Quincey
Lewis Carroll	R. L. Stevenson	Thomas Dixon
Lewis Sperry Chafer	R. S. Ball	Thomas H. Huxley
Lilian Bell	Rabindranath Tagore	Thomas Hardy
Lloyd Osbourne	Rahul Alvares	Thomas More
Louis Hughes	Ralph Bonehill	Thornton W. Burgess
Louis Joseph Vance	Ralph Henry Barbour	U. S. Grant
Louis Tracy	Ralph Victor	Upton Sinclair
Louisa May Alcott	Ralph Waldo Emmerson	Valentine Williams
Lucy Fitch Perkins	Rene Descartes	Various Authors
Lucy Maud Montgomery	Ray Cummings	Vaughan Kester
Luther Benson	Rex Beach	Victor Appleton
Lydia Miller Middleton	Rex E. Beach	Victor G. Durham
Lyndon Orr	Richard Harding Davis	Victoria Cross
M. Corvus	Richard Jefferies	Virginia Woolf
M. H. Adams	Richard Le Gallienne	Wadsworth Camp
Margaret E. Sangster	Robert Barr	Walter Camp
Margret Howth	Robert Frost	Walter Scott
Margaret Vandercook	Robert Gordon Anderson	Washington Irving
Margaret W. Hungerford	Robert L. Drake	Wilbur Lawton
Margret Penrose	Robert Lansing	Wilkie Collins
Maria Edgeworth	Robert Lynd	Willa Cather
Maria Thompson Daviess	Robert Michael Ballantyne	Willard F. Baker
Mariano Azuela	Robert W. Chambers	William Dean Howells
Marion Polk Angellotti	Rosa Nouchette Carey	William le Queux
Mark Overton	Rudyard Kipling	W. Makepeace Thackeray
Mark Twain	Saint Augustine	William W. Walter
Mary Austin	Samuel B. Allison	William Shakespeare
Mary Catherine Crowley	Samuel Hopkins Adams	Winston Churchill
Mary Cole	Sarah Bernhardt	Yei Theodora Ozaki
Mary Hastings Bradley	Sarah C. Hallowell	Yogi Ramacharaka
Mary Roberts Rinehart	Selma Lagerlof	Young E. Allison
Mary Rowlandson	Sherwood Anderson	Zane Grey
M. Wollstonecraft Shelley	Sigmund Freud	
Maud Lindsay	Standish O'Grady	
Max Beerbohm	Stanley Weyman	
Myra Kelly	Stella Benson	
Nathaniel Hawthrone	Stella M. Francis	
Nicolo Machiavelli	Stephen Crane	
O. F. Walton	Stewart Edward White	
Oscar Wilde	Stijn Streuvels	
Owen Johnson	Swami Abhedananda	
P.G. Wodehouse	Swami Parmananda	
Paul and Mabel Thorne	T. S. Ackland